The Esoteric World of Chakras

Dedication and Acknowledgments

I gratefully dedicate this book to my spiritual master MahaVajra, whose teachings comprise the majority of the project.

I am also grateful for the moral support and assistance of my talented friends, Richela Chapman and Simon Lacouline. Richela performed the editing and is a spiritual teacher, healer and author. Simon created the images in the book content; he is a webmaster and author. And finally, gratitude to Mauricio Pastor for creating the cover art.

ISBN 978-1-926659-24-4
F.Lepine Publishing
Copyright Cori Leach © 2014

Table of Contents

Introduction 5
Chakras and Spiritual Practice 7
   Meditation Techniques 8
      What is Meditation 8
      Transcending 9
      What is a Mantra 9
      What is a Mala 10
      Japa 10
   Emotional Integration 13
   The 21 Masks of the Ego 17

The Chakra 23
   What is a Chakra 25
      Human and Vital Energy 25
         Introduction to Nadis 28
         Awakening Kundalini 29
         Common Associations of the Chakras 30
      Soul and Consciousness 32
      Divine and Universal Consciousness 34
   Contemplations on the VishwaChakra 35
      The Vishnu Shiva Cycle 35
      The Four Siddhis 37
      Quantum Metaphysics 39
      The Lord's Prayer 40
      The Convection Mantra 42
      Meditation on the VishwaChakra 43

Spiritual Practices with Individual Chakras 45
Introduction 47
Hindu and Buddhist Meditation 49
Chakra Mandalas 51
The Ten Planes of Consciousness 59
Five Elements of Creation 63
R'shiNaya 69
Kuji-In 73
The Cauldron Technique 85
Kabbalistic Meditation 87
The Archangels 89
The YEOUAN Technique 97

Summary by Chakra 99
Base 101
Sacral 102
Dan Tian 103
Solar Plexus 104
Heart 105
Throat 106
Third Eye 107
Jade Gate 108
Crown 109

Conclusion 111

References 113

Introduction

As with many natural healers and others on the spiritual path, I often find myself contemplating chakras. Universally accepted generic information can be found just about anywhere:

- The Sanskrit word chakra means "wheel", or "perpetual motion"
- The chakra is a vortex of energy that is part of the structure of energy pathways in the body
- Each chakra is associated with particular body structures and functions, as well as emotional and mental states of being
- Dis-ease of body, mind or heart influences the balance of the chakras, and vice-versa
- The intensity of energy at each chakra can be physically felt by the hands of energy workers, and so chakras are the focus points for energy healing and for spiritual meditations

In my own Reiki practice I could see that the associations between chakras and body/mind/heart did, for the most part, seem to support what I had been told by my teachers and fellow healers, or had read somewhere. But I wanted to know WHY, and I wanted to know from a spiritual point of view.

Esoteric mysticism basically refers to selectively shared (originally secret) practices that nurture conscious awareness of spiritual truth. I am blessed to have received many perspectives on chakras from a variety of spiritual teachings. This book is an attempt to weave together the treasures of these teachings, and perhaps gently guide you to your own truth of the underlying essence of the chakra through spiritual experiences. The content is not meant to be all-inclusive, only what I've been exposed to in the last few years. Every perception is Truth, and yet none is completely Truth—each is a tool to accomplish a desired goal.

Reading this book will expose you to esoteric contemplations and meditations and the techniques with which to practice them. If you allow yourself to be vulnerable and sink into the teachings, allowing the consciousness to truly touch you, you will gain real wisdom. Real wisdom in not just knowledge and technique; it is what results from experience. Wisdom leads to the transformation of your perception—Awakening.

What is presented here is not in any way intended to be initiation or complete teaching—this requires interaction with a competent master. Rather, it is an overview to activate expanded contemplation.

Chakras and Spiritual Practice

Most of us are first exposed to chakras as energetic areas in the body used by energy healers to assist physical healing. The intensity and consistency of the chakra vibration can be an indication of physical dis-ease. While energy work with a chakra can have a positive effect on dis-ease, dis-ease is a manifestation of suffering caused by our emotions. Treatment by an energy healer has a temporary effect until we can look inside and purify our emotions. This purification is spiritual evolution.

Each of us is a divine incarnation of God. Inherent in this truth is separation, because in our incarnation as a human we naturally perceive from a point of view of isolation. This perception manifests as states of being which arise from reactions to the experience of events and relationships in our lives. And these states of being are woven into the essence of chakras.

If you visualize each chakra as an organ of perception of the soul, you will see the chakra continually bringing information about particular varieties of experience from Human to Spirit and back again to Human. Each chakra has lessons of its own, and this book is designed to introduce you to the experience of the lessons through various forms of meditation. The effort of learning our life lessons, of elevating our perception and thus our happiness, results in evolution.

Meditation Techniques

You can find the following techniques in many forms of spiritual practice as they are efficient methods for those on a spiritual path. I've included some guidance here because they are essential to receive the most benefit from your exploration of the chakras.

What is Meditation?

Meditation is paying attention and altering your state of being. The goal is to empower your Self, your Soul, so much that your spiritual consciousness overrides your human identity for a few moments. Next are simple steps for the most basic meditation, which is done best in silence—both physically and in the mind.

1. Sit and breathe, paying attention to your breath.
2. Pay attention to yourself, inside.
3. Calm and clear your mind. Clearing your mind of thoughts cannot be done by pushing them away; it is the absence of effort. If you are looking at a blue sky and birds fly across your view, keep your attention on the sky. Ripples on the surface of a pond will settle by themselves. Don't put any energy into not thinking.
4. Observe that you are aware of yourself. This is Self-awareness, or Consciousness.

So we sit, relax, and pay attention inside. We aren't used to paying attention to the same thing for more than a few seconds. If there is no change—if there doesn't seem to be movement, sounds or variations—our mind will try to pay attention to something else, hoping to be stimulated. When you notice that your mind is wandering, softly bring your attention back inside. At this point you might have an additional goal in your meditation such as contemplation, or sinking into states of being. (This book includes an in-depth section on each technique mentioned in the following paragraphs.)

If you want to contemplate a spiritual philosophy for deeper understanding and possible revelation, review what you want to contemplate, do the four basic meditation steps, and simply allow information to come. If you actively think about it, your mind could filter or alter the Truth. This is a good way to contemplate the chakra mandalas (the lotus images which represent chakras), the meaning of the VishwaChakra (the Universal Chakra—feeling the turning of the chakra as one cosmic experience), or the Lord's Prayer. But often, we softly repeat a mantra (a phrase to bring a state of being) along with the contemplation. We will use this technique when contemplating the Siddhis (powers, or accomplishments) or doing the R'shiNaya (Hindu holy path) process. This is passive meditation.

Meditation can also be more active in nature. Japa is a type of meditation in which one uses a mala (a prayer necklace) to count while chanting mantras and contemplating (see the section on Japa below).

An example of this would be meditating on the Five Elements. Kuji-In is a complex meditation, using mudras (hand positions), mantras, focus on a chakra, an energy visualization, and contemplation of spiritual philosophy.

Transcending

When you meditate it is possible that you will "transcend". It might seem as if you lost consciousness, or went to sleep. But transcending is the awakening of your consciousness, and before you become used to it, this shuts down the human experience for short periods. The human seems to sleep because the level of energy and information at the spiritual level of the Self is so intense that it's a little overwhelming.

This is the goal of every technique of transcendental meditation. In a transcendent state of consciousness, you are fully free of your human limitations. You are cleansing your soul, expanding, refilling with light and pure thought.

After years of practice, a time will come when you will transcend, but remain conscious of what is going on even in a state of expanded consciousness. When you return to your normal state of consciousness, you will also retain some level of memory of what happened to you during your transcendental experience.

What is a Mantra?

A mantra is a series of words that are formulated to lead us to an experience, altering our state of consciousness. A mantra itself has no power; it's the experience that has the power. When a mantra seems to address a deity (a god or goddess) we are invoking the state of being of that deity—for example, the Fire mantra of the Five Elements invokes radiance and purification by addressing Goddess Agni. Saying a mantra out loud brings the feeling of the mantra into the body, even to the level of genetic code. You may recite the mantra as fast as you want, but it must be intelligible.

I chant mantras in Sanskrit rather than English or other contemporary languages. Hebrew and Sanskrit are two languages that were created to vibrationally represent as accurately as possible the experience of a pure thought. Each letter has its own meaning, so a word has many layers of vibration in consciousness. "Om" is a meaningless word. But if the divine concept of "everything" could be sounded by a human voice, it would be Om. Also, if we were to use English, we would be speaking words that we use every day in a common, non-sacred attitude. If you are speaking in English, it's easier for your mind to wander to your daily human experience. We use Sanskrit only when we are in a sacred practice. So the moment we begin reciting mantras, "Om..." the mind connects to the Self.

What is a Mala?

The mala is a string of beads, usually with a tassel, used when reciting mantras, or prayers, similar to a Catholic rosary. Beads are typically crafted from seeds, wood, bone or stone. The most common mala is a necklace of 108 beads—a very auspicious number. The numerological meaning of 108 is "the realization (8) of primordial consciousness (1) in the world (0), aiming at perfection (1+0+8=9). Some Hindu necklaces have 109 beads, (the extra bead is used to hold the tassel, but is not counted.) Malas can also be in the form of a bracelet, and have 21 or 27 beads.

Japa

A powerful way to receive the consciousness of a mantra is to do japa, meaning that we will chant (repeatedly speak) a certain mantra 108 times while using the mala to count. It is a means of counting without placing too much attention on the counting. This allows us to focus on the philosophy and visualization of the mantras, and it also transforms the mala into a power item—a tool we can use to augment our spiritual or healing activities because it is infused with some of the consciousness from the mantra we chanted.

MALA TECHNIQUE—using the right hand, begin the counting with the first bead *after* the bead with the tassel. This bead will be "1", and the tassel bead will be "108". "Roll the mala", or "pop a bead" with either the thumb or major (middle) finger. Using your index finger to shift the beads will empty the charge. This emptying occurs because of the meaning of the index finger, which can vary from one meditation style to another. It could represent human ego (whose effect can diminish our state of consciousness), or represent the fire element (which burns and purifies)—either way, the index finger removes the charge of our mantras. However, it is perfectly okay to touch the mala with the index while not doing japa.

Hold the mala with both hands, creating a loose loop. If counting with the right thumb (the most common method), hold hands with palms up, mala resting on ring fingers. Pull the mala toward you with the right thumb. If counting with the major finger, hold your hands palms down with the tips of thumbs and ring fingers touching, and the mala resting where they touch. Pull the mala toward you with the right major finger. Choose whichever method is most comfortable for you. You can also roll the mala with just the right hand, leaving the left hand free or positioned in a mudra (hand gesture) of your choice.

THE TASSEL—the original meaning of the tassel was simply practical—to mark the 108th bead as a counter. But it carries the significance of "energy that flows from consciousness". At the end of each mala, touch the tassel to the 3rd eye to signify oneness with divinity. You can also touch the tassel to the right eye, then left eye, then 3rd eye, for seeing this divinity everywhere. Either way, the result will be the same—we put ourselves in communion with our preferred divinity.

GUIDELINES FOR CHARGING MANTRAS: THE 9 X 12 FORMULA—there isn't an absolutely required rule on how to charge mantras; we are charging consciousness, and this is always perfect. But there is a recommended time frame—9 malas (or 35 minutes) for 12 consecutive days. This formula is a guarantee to raise consciousness. But you can do 3 malas per day for 36 consecutive days, or 1 mala per day for 108 consecutive days, as each formula results in 108 malas. We can use a muscle-building analogy—a manageable amount of sacrifice for an extended time is the best balance (9 x 12) and gives the best results.

If you want to do more than 9 malas per day, it's best to just charge several different mantras. Do all nine malas of one mantra, then do nine malas of the next mantra. If you must miss a day, try to do one mala to hold the energy, and add a day at the end of the 12 days.

If you transcended or fell asleep during a charge, you were still activating the energy prior to transcendence or sleep. If you didn't finish the charge on this day, just don't count the day. Upon coming back to normal awareness, do a few mantras to prevent the process from being lost and add a day at the end of the 12 days.

USING A MALA AS A POWER ITEM—when you want to use the power for yourself, wear a wrist mala on your left wrist (left signifies passive or receiving). If it's for healing, wear it on your right wrist (right signifies active or giving)—the energy that flows through your hand resonates with the charge. A necklace-style mala is worn around the neck for either purpose, but can be looped several times around your wrist if you choose.

WEARING YOUR MALA—when you wear a charged mala, it elevates your energy. Wear it to encourage energies, or when you feel spiritual. Wear it constantly if you want to be spiritual all day, and don't wear it when you don't want to be spiritual. The more you wear it when spiritual, the more it affects you—both you and the mala elevate back to the state when you were charging it. When not wearing it, you may place the mala on the surface of your altar or you can keep it in a small pouch or case. It's best not to leave it out in sunlight or moonlight, as we use this technique when we want to purify the malas.

Emotional Integration

What is Emotional Integration?

Emotional integration is a meditation which relieves the suffering of our emotions. It doesn't prevent us from having emotions—rather, it provides a method to observe our emotions and live without drama. We follow four steps—we breathe, pay attention inside our body to our emotions, allow ourselves to fully feel and suffer those emotions, and then observe them until they dissolve. At the end of this we force ourselves to be happy ☺

This is conscious suffering—we choose to consciously suffer today, so that we don't suffer in the future.

Wisdom

Our thoughts and emotions are of the body, not of the soul. We experience pain and pleasure as part of our human awareness—they are the result of physical reactions (nerve firings and hormonal changes) to external influences which we perceive as good or bad. But the Soul perceives these events without judgment—they are just experiences.

The Soul brings the events and relationships (and our resulting human experiences of happiness and suffering) to our lives as part of our path to enlightenment. We (at the level of Soul) ask for everything. But it's natural that we forget about this, and spend a lot of energy resisting what feels difficult and unpleasant. We often turn to an outside experience to distract ourselves from the suffering, such as spending time with friends, playing video games, or eating our favorite food. But every time we resist a lesson, the Soul continues to find a way to bring the experience. If we ignore the lesson when it manifests at a small level, the Soul brings the experience again, at a more intense level.

Three Major Families of Emotion

The three major families of emotion are guilt, rejection and abandonment; other emotions fall under these categories (see the next section on the 21 Masks of the Ego for an explanation about the emotions). For example, if we are angry, it might be because we feel rejected by our children when they don't follow our advice. Grief over the death of a loved one, or divorce, may be the result of abandonment. Fear relates to all three families. Tracing emotions back to one of these three efficiently gets to the root of suffering.

The Four States of Being

(See the section on the Ten Planes of Consciousness for wisdom of the planes mentioned here.)

1. Breathe (Affects the Physical plane)
   Breathe deeply. Don't force the exhale, just let go and let it flow naturally, all the way out. Pay attention to the feel of the breath in your body and be at peace. Continue conscious breathing throughout the process.

2. Inhabit (Affects the Vital plane) Vital energy is the subtle energy which provides us life. See the section on Human and Vital energy.
   Pay attention to your body and your emotions. Be aware of an emotion you feel, or have felt lately. If you can trace it back to abandonment, rejection or guilt, good. If you can't that's okay. Breathe in the experience.

3. Feel (Affects the Emotional plane)
   Sit in the emotion. Try to be vulnerable, and don't resist the emotion. Allow yourself to feel so deeply that you become the emotion. Let the emotion overwhelm you; even crush you if it is quite intense. Pay attention only to the emotion, not to where your mind might try to take you—don't analyze it, justify it, or try to find any solutions. Just breathe the pain. For a moment at the end of each exhale, find peace. Eventually, this peace begins to seep into the entire breath.

4. Observe (Affects the Mental plane)
   Observe yourself feeling this emotion. You still feel the emotion, but you become less and less attached to it. It's like watching someone else in a movie—you feel compassion, but you're not suffering so much. The pain starts to dissolve. *If we pay attention to something long enough, it becomes consciousness.* Observe until the suffering dissolves.

These four steps are done at the same time as one event. Breathe in the emotion, inhabit it, feel it, observe it.

For most of us, it's best to begin with something small, so that we can experience success. Do this process until the emotion dissolves. The suffering you carry could be so heavy that the emotion won't dissolve in one sitting—that's okay. You could stop after 30 minutes or so if you don't feel progress, but remember to do the happy facing described below. Even if you don't feel it, you are making a difference; it's like moving a mountain one teaspoon at a time. And you are also training your ego to take direction from you.

As you go through the process, you might remember other events when you felt the same emotion. Jot them down briefly; work on these experiences another time.

Generate Happiness!

It is very important to finish up the integration session by feeling happy! This is not the kind of happiness that is dependent on outside experiences, but pure happiness that you create just because you want it. Imagine that your Heart chakra (in the center of your chest) is a giant yellow smiley face, and that all of the blood cells flowing through your veins are smiley faces. They are so happy! They vibrate, jumping up and down with joy. They flow through you and up and out of your crown chakra, creating a fountain of happy faces that swirls around your body. Smile! Put your arms around yourself and hug yourself, and tell yourself "I love you". This feels good now, and also encourages the ego to cooperate next time we do integration.

Following Up

Integrating Similar Emotional Responses

You just freed yourself from a suffering related to a particular event or relationship. Now, you can work on preventing suffering in the future by integrating other events with the same emotion attached to it—the ones you remembered during the current session. We learn from our earliest moments of life to have particular emotional responses to events, but we can break this conditioning with integration. The next time a similar event occurs, we attach little or no drama to it. We release our attachment to emotions tied to the past, and thus release our attachment to emotions that will arise in the future.

Integration Creates Power

The ultimate expression of power is vulnerability. When we suffer everything through integration, the power of events over our emotions dissolves away. A good example of this can be found in martial arts. If an opponent pushes against you to move you off your center and you forcibly resist, your resistance gives your opponent power over you. However, if you take one step to the side, without resisting, your opponent's own force guides him past you, throwing him off balance.

It also follows naturally that your power over others increases without you having to do or say anything. Many times people react negatively to us because at a deep level they feel our guilt, rejection or abandonment. Others want to be loved, and our feelings can spark a need in them to "protect" themselves. Your higher level of consciousness, the simple happiness of trusting life, manifests a positive effect on events and people in your life.

21 Masks of the Ego

The 21 Masks of the Ego are a tool to help us identify and understand our emotions so that emotional integration becomes more efficient.

Soul and Ego

In the beginning there was only God, which can be described as Void. There was only Oneness, and then God forced Himself into Separation so that He could experience Love in the form of interaction. Creation was born from Separation, but what is created is still pure God, made of Love. So the Soul is completely God from a localized or individual point of view. However, the Soul can perceive Oneness.

The Ego is also made of God. Ego is our awareness of and reaction to Separation. Through Ego we experience the illusion of not being loved by God, we forget we are made of Love. This part of us holds on tight to the belief in Separation, causing joyful and painful emotions to rise up inside us as we search for love outside of ourselves. The Ego is a tool, a beautiful gift, the contrast that shows us the light of God. If we can learn to observe and master our emotions, we learn that all is Love. The conscious dance between the Ego and the Soul brings us this understanding.

The 21 Masks of the Ego guide us in looking at our emotions and behaviors so that we can identify and understand the forces of nature inside ourselves.

~ Never forget that as we observe, forgiveness is essential. ~

~ Understanding is a tool, but the objective is to feel. ~

21 Masks of the Ego

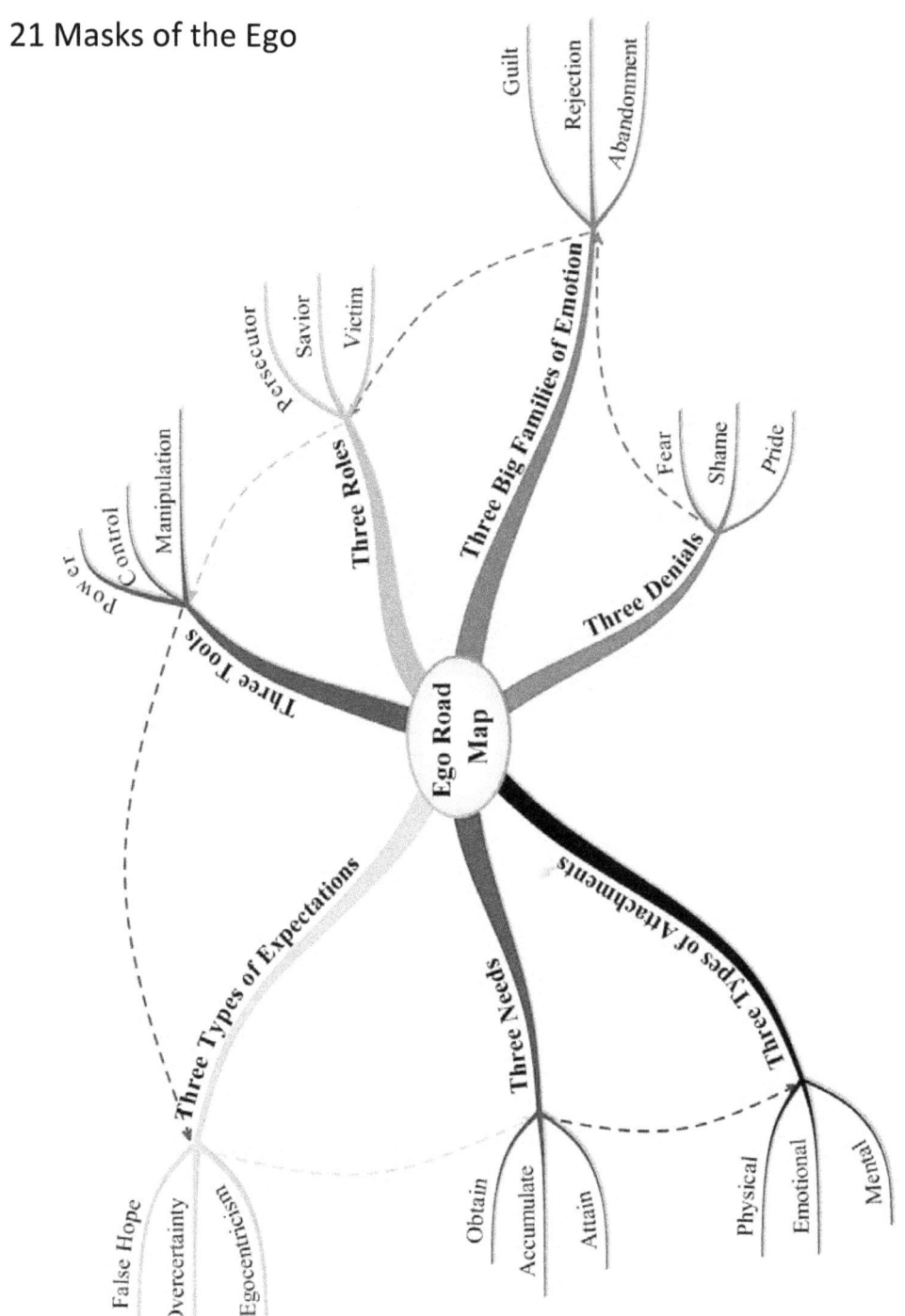

The Three Denials

Denial means to choose our perception of life from the point of view of Ego rather than Soul.

Fear is avoidance. We don't want to suffer, and fear helps us avoid painful experiences or even survive. We want to be with another person, but don't ask for a date because of fear of rejection. We don't apply for jobs because we fear no one will want to hire us (rejection), or that we won't be competent and will be fired (abandonment).

Pride is the most obvious and complicated of the denials. Pride is a lie—we pretend that we are in charge, and that we don't suffer from emotions. We justify our mistakes. We use pride to protect our image—to others and to ourselves. Pride grows from a profound need for outside love. We say or do things to compete or get attention in some form. The mask of Pride can be self-sustaining—we are proud of being proud. Not feeling important or being "right" can generate self-hatred; thus pride leads us to shame.

Shame is feeling unlovable. When we try to show how good we are, and no one responds, we sink in shame. We isolate, not wanting to expose ourselves and receive either negative or no attention at all. We feel very alone.

The Three Emotions

The Soul experiences emotion not as "good" or "bad", but as pure experience. The Soul doesn't perceive the distinction between emotions, but the Ego sees the distinction and even classifies it into many variations. These are the main categories:

Abandonment is when something went away, and we feel alone. A relationship can change in the form of physical death or a breakup. We can lose a job, or a car, or anything. Something could leave us, or *we* could leave—it is all abandonment.

Rejection is when someone or something pushes us away, or doesn't love us in the way that we want to be loved. Someone could call us an asshole, or the IRS might conduct an audit. We could push something away. When we find our own self to be unlovable, that is a form of rejection.

Guilt doesn't rise up because we did something wrong; it depends on our perception of whether or not others approve of what we did (or didn't do). If we did the right thing, but others judge us, then we feel guilty. A student could study hard for a test and make a high score that skews the bell curve for other students (his friends)—they then blame the good student for their lower scores, and he feels guilty. If we do something "wrong" but others are happy about it, we don't feel guilty. For example, a gang member commits a crime as part of his gang initiation, and everyone congratulates him.

Existential guilt is the guilt of being alive. We love God so much but feel our separation from Him, projecting that God doesn't love us.

The Three Roles

Roles are behaviors we exhibit as an attempt to alleviate our suffering from the three emotions.

The Persecutor applies power to resolve the pain of abandonment or rejection. Usually a persecutor doesn't actively try to hurt another, but acts with indifference.

The Savior helps others in order to receive something—love in return. The reward could be attention or a feeling of worthiness—usually from others, but it could also be from yourself. Sometimes the savior wants the victim to remain a victim, so he can keep his savior role and the victim can continue to give him credit. The savior cannot peacefully accept to let others live their experiences (karma) and evolve.

The Victim complains and makes sure someone knows when he suffers in order to get attention from others and feel loved. Even in victim we can play the role of persecutor in our complaining, such as complaining about government and politicians. Sometimes the savior plays the victim, complaining he has so much to do for others.

The Three Tools

We use tools to apply force while playing the roles. Tools can all be good and helpful. However, when we can't accept that another doesn't love us the way we want, we try to force them to act in a way that will prove their love to us. In this way, using the tools is a detrimental influence on the free will of others.

Power is a single act of strong expression. We impose ourselves on others to take what we want, or to produce happiness. The problem is that we can become addicted to power, usually because of pride. A parent uses power when giving a child a quick swat to teach them not to do something dangerous.

Control means applying continuous force in a systemized way. Control can be useful—it helps us be aware and responsible. Control becomes a problem when we feel the *need* to control, whether or not it is required to attain a result. One usually uses control when power isn't enough. A parent uses control when grounding a child for a period of time.

Manipulation is making another believe that they will gain a benefit by doing what we want. We use manipulation (usually in a sneaky or subtle manner) when power and control don't produce the results we want, or when we want to protect our role as a helpless victim by invoking guilt in others. We express manipulation by being agile in our actions or arguments.

The Three Expectations

Expectations are outcomes we hope for related to a specific event or experience. This is different from the virtue of Hope, which is a universal feeling that everything will always be fine.

False Hope is a feeling that everything will turn out as we wish even though deep down we know it is impossible, or almost impossible. Maybe we still expect an ex-lover to return to us when he is now happily married to another. Or we count on winning the lottery when the odds are 2 million to 1.

Overcertainty means thinking we have control of everything to turn out the way we want, without needing to be prudent or wise. The expectation of overcertainty is not objective; it is careless and takes things for granted. One could lie on their tax return, feeling that there is absolutely no chance the IRS would conduct an audit.

Egocentrism is thinking that all the importance of a situation revolves around us. It is a certainty that everything is about us and for us, without caring about the welfare of others. In egocentrism we express greed and lack of care about the karmic influences of our actions. We observe egocentrism when someone at the grocery store with an overflowing basket rushes and pushes to get in line ahead of someone with only a few items. Thinking that another is egocentric arises from the rejection and pride of our own egocentrism.

The Three Needs

The needs are the expressions of getting something for our self. Needs can be very constructive in our lives unless they become addictive in nature or go against the free will of another. If others remain happy and their needs fulfilled, it is emotionally healthy to fill our needs and practice non-attachment. Non-attachment is enjoying what we have (or here, what we are attempting to have), but choosing to be happy if we don't have them.

Obtaining means acquiring something needed or wanted. Satisfying this need is most often related to a physical object, such as purchasing a pair of shoes.

Accumulating is obtaining more and more resources when we already have enough, and is mostly driven by emotional needs. Driven by the feeling of dissatisfaction rather than contentment, we feel the need to have thirty pairs of shoes.

Attaining, or achieving, means reaching an objective, which is mental in nature. It can be caused by or lead to self-infatuation. Satisfying this need could be expressed by working toward a college degree, getting a promotion at work, or writing a book.

The Three Attachments

We cause ourselves suffering when we lose things to which we are attached. We even suffer when we have those things, imagining the suffering that will rise when we no longer have them. It is wise to enjoy something when we have it, conscious of and accepting that everything is impermanent, so that we can be happy when that thing or person goes away—this is non-attachment. Still, we can be prudent and responsible about maintaining the objects of our non-attachment (make your car payment if possible).

Physical attachments are mostly related to possessions. I would suffer if I lost my car.

Emotional attachments are mostly related to relationships. I would suffer if my lover left, or if my teenage child began to hate me.

Mental attachments are mostly related to identity, and are closely bound to pride. I would suffer if I had the lowest test score in the class.

All these experiences of the ego are about wanting to feel loved. The power of love drives us. We feel abandoned, rejected and guilty because we want to feel loved. We play the roles of persecutor, victim and savior using the force of power, control, and manipulation because we want to be loved. We have hopes of being loved; we fill our needs, and become attached to what we believe will make us feel loved. And we prevent ourselves from seeing all of this through fear, pride and shame. Observe and forgive both yourself and others. It's natural, we are made this way. But with integration we can master ourselves.

The Chakra

What is a Chakra?

What are these mystical chakras? The essence of the chakra is multi-dimensional—they are made of vital energy (the energy in our body that gives life), and we experience them at the physical, vital, emotional and mental level of our human existence. This human experience is the most evident, as we might physically feel heat and vibration, see colors, and benefit from stress and pain relief as the result of a treatment performed by an energy healer.

The chakras are also present and influential where the distinction between our human and soul perception fades away, and even in the part of us that is divine in nature. Each of us experience in the chakras what we are looking for. We feel them based on our goal—healing, self-introspection, evolution...or all of these.

Human and Vital Energy

From the common and prevalent viewpoint of physical energy, chakras draw universal life force energy into and through our bodies. Chakra is a Sanskrit word meaning "constantly turning". As part of the vital structure of the tens-to-hundreds of thousands of energy pathways in the body, the energy forms vortexes—these vortexes are the chakras, the Energy Gates of the body. The spinning motion draws the universal life force energy rather like a stream into and through the body from the moment of conception; it is this energy that supports life.

Universal life force energy is what makes up, flows through, and connects all things. Imagine this energy as the ocean, and our bodies as fishing nets in that ocean. There is no containment, no separation, of the water inside one fishing net from the water outside that fishing net. Neither is there separation of the water in one fishing net from the water in another fishing net. Now imagine a few small fish in a net. Even though the net is filled with water, and the fish are composed mainly of water, the fish need a fresh flow of water from outside the net, constantly moving through the net, to stay in perfect health. The flowing water brings nutrients and oxygen, but also removes the waste naturally created by the metabolism of the fish.

We can compare the fish to the cells of our bodies. The cells need a constant flow of energy from the universe around us to flush out the dis-ease created by the physical and emotional stress that results from the natural process of living.

The major chakras are the areas where energy most powerfully enters the body and where we physically feel it most intensely ("intensely" is a comparative word, as most people feel the energy as very subtle). As healers, we feel it on the surface of the body, or a few inches above it, and this is where we place our hands for efficient energy treatments. When meditating, we feel it inside our body.

There are several schools of thought about the number of major chakras. The following image shows the location of the eight major chakras. The most widely accepted interpretation recognizes seven major chakras—it excludes the Jade Gate because it is thought to be the back of the 3rd Eye chakra. But the experiential associations of the Jade Gate are quite different than the 3rd Eye. The major chakras are aligned in an ascending column from the base of the spine to the top of the head and correspond to the endocrine system. And the Sushumna, or Central Channel, extends from the Base to the Crown, connecting all the major chakras.

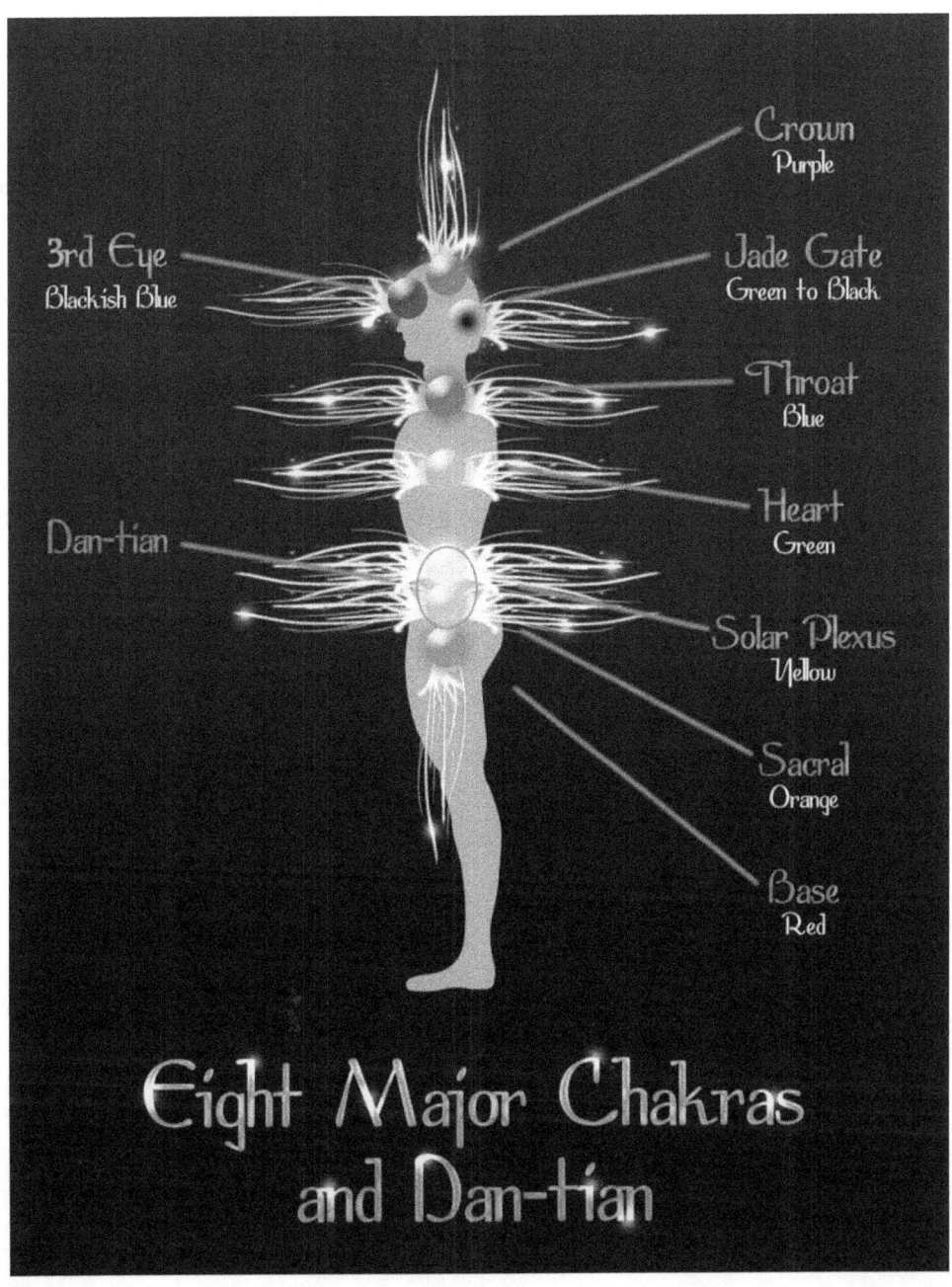

We also have minor chakras at all of the major joints, as well as the soles of the feet and the palms of the hands. The New Age practice of associating colors of the rainbow with chakras represents the range of energy frequencies from lowest frequency at the Base chakra to highest frequency at the Crown—most physical at the base to most spiritual at the Crown. Many people experience different patterns of color when giving or receiving energy treatments.

Introduction to Nadis

The Sanskrit term nadi comes from the root nad, meaning "motion". A nadi is a current in the vital or astral body along which the prana (vital force) resonates—the energy pathways we've been talking about. Various ancient sources tell us that there are between 72,000 and 350,000 nadis; the primary nadis are Ida, Pingala and Sushumna, which reside in the torso and head.

Sushumna (meaning most gracious) is also known as the Central Channel and extends along the spinal column from the Base chakra to the Crown chakra. The Ida (also known as Chandra, or Moon nadi) resonates along the right side of Sushumna, and Pingala (also known as Surya, or Sun nadi) resonates alongside the left. The common teaching expresses that Ida and Pingala first meet Sushumna Nadi at the Base chakra, then wind back and forth, continuing to intersect with Sushumna to form a vortex which becomes each major Chakra, until they meet and end at Ajna (3rd Eye) Chakra. This was the experience of the first holy people who recorded it, and how most images depict it. The section on Chakra Mandalas gives a detailed contemplation of the symbols representing the chakras.

7 Major Chakras with Sushumna, Ida and Pingala

Awakening Kundalini

I include a simple introduction to Kundalini here because of its unmentioned relationship to many topics in this book, and because most people want to know about sexual energies. Kundalini is divine level experience at the human level. Kundalini is not energy as is commonly taught, but an experience; I explain it like energy because it makes it easier to visualize and understand. Chakras are also not just energy flow, but experience—this concept is discussed more fully in the section on Soul and Consciousness.

Prana (vital energy) begins its path along Ida and Pingala, entering the body between the eyebrows. It flows up inside and following the curve of the skull, and then follows all the nerve systems down along the spine. As energy densifies, these two channels naturally fill up. Where they meet at the Base chakra, the energy condenses, collides, and mixes. This represents the copulation of the masculine and feminine aspects, the reuniting of yin and yang as the one consciousness. The sexual energy in your body is the Creator, Kundalini power, wrapped tight and desiring to awaken.

How can we awaken Kundalini? We use spiritual practice as a tool to help us become aware of and nourish the power of God inside us, and to fall into the enormous simplicity of being in love with God. The Holy Trinity exists in the body as Sushumna, Ida and Pingala. Awaken the consciousness of the God the Creator, or Brahma. Sing "Halleluiah" to celebrate Buddhahood, Vishnu, and Christ. Chant "Om Namah Shivaya" or a prayer to the Holy Ghost. Pray, and then bring the consciousness of what you feel into your body—this will awaken your Kundalini.

When Kundalini awakens, the experience of presence and pure embodiment builds pressure and begins to push; the manifested energy in the Base chakra begins to vibrate and moves up inside your body. As it encounters the resonating force of the Sacral chakra, then the Solar Plexus, and so on, it simply flows around the chakras. The energy doesn't crisscross back and forth, and it doesn't intersect or create the chakras—we simply feel the side effect of the movement around the chakras. It's not even a fixed waving channel of energy; it just flows up, unstructured. We feel the Kundalini energy different ways—sometimes we feel the radiance and transformation like snakes intertwining; sometimes we feel energy flowing up and down the spine at the same time, or everywhere; and sometimes we feel it polarizing and dancing around the chakras.

When the energy flows we feel great pressure. It can cause quite a bit of pain in the groin, the Solar Plexus (front and back), heart, the lungs, the throat, the Jade Gate, and the Third Eye. We experience purification and expanding consciousness as energy flows out of the Third Eye. Finally this energy fills the head and pours like a powerful fountain out of the Crown chakra, going back from whence it came.

Common Associations of the Chakras

Each chakra has associations with certain aspects of our planes of existence—our physical, vital, emotional and mental levels (see the Ten Planes of Consciousness section). On the physical level, each is associated with things near to it, but also with structures that span the entire body. A physical dis-ease is a manifestation of mental or emotional dis-ease and reminds us to go inside and observe ourselves with compassion and forgiveness. Practicing the very efficient technique of emotional Integration brings emotional healing, which should be done along with any required medical treatments.

Following are commonly accepted (meaning you can find similar information in various websites and books) emotional/mental issues and physical associations of the seven major chakras. The teaching on Jade Gate is not commonly accepted. Each section will end with the primary spiritual lesson available to us through the spiritual practice found later in this book.

The Base chakra (also known as Muladhara chakra, the Root chakra, or the 1st chakra) is located just inside the perineum—the soft area between the sexual organs and anus—and is represented by the color red. At the emotional/mental level, it is associated with our survival and need for security and trust. These issues influence the skeletal (and locally the tailbone area), lymph and elimination systems. The main spiritual lesson comes from allowing faith to overcome fear.

The Sacral chakra (also known as Svadhishthana chakra, Hara, Water chakra, or 2nd chakra) is located 2-3 inches below the navel, and is represented by the color orange. At the emotional/mental level, it is associated with our adaptability to change, to our appetite for outside comforts—food, sex, drugs, mental stimulation, material things—and to creativity (or pro-creativity). These issues influence the low back and the reproductive and assimilation systems, including the bladder. The main spiritual lesson comes from allowing self-mastery to overcome karma. (Karma is our current life experience which results from past actions, words, and thoughts.)

The Dan-tian is not a chakra, but an energy area located inside the abdomen whose center is located behind the navel—it encompasses the entire bowel system. Chi is gathered and stored in the dan-tian for use by the body. The main spiritual lesson comes from allowing self-observation to overcome drama.

The Solar Plexus chakra (also known as Manipura chakra or 3rd chakra) is located between the bottom of the rib cage and the navel, and is represented by the color yellow. At the emotional/mental level, it is associated with our sense of will power, self-confidence, competition, and with the emotions of power—anger and joy. These issues influence the stomach, the liver, the gall bladder, the spleen, the pancreas, and the mid-back. Further, they affect the entire digestive system, the muscle system, and the circulation of insulin throughout the body. The main spiritual lesson comes from allowing kindness to master power.

The Heart chakra (also known as Anahata chakra or 4th chakra) is located at the level of the physical heart, but along the midline, and is represented by the color green. At the emotional/mental level, it is associated with our judgment and our ability to feel compassion for others and ourselves. These issues influence the respiration, circulation and immune systems (thymus gland). The main spiritual lesson comes from allowing compassion to overcome the suffering of human love.

The Throat chakra (also known as Vishuddha chakra or 5th chakra) is located at the base of the throat, and is represented by a medium blue color. At the emotional/mental level, it is associated with many layers of communication—listening to others, expressing ourselves to others, and listening to our inner voice. These issues influence our throat, neck, vocal apparatus and metabolism (thyroid gland). The main spiritual lesson is that truth (experience) transforms knowledge.

The Third Eye chakra (also known as Ajna chakra or 6th chakra) is located between the eyebrows, and is represented by the color indigo (blackish-blue). At the emotional/mental level, it is associated with clarity of mind and manifestation. These issues influence eye, nose, ears, the entire endocrine system (as affected by the pituitary gland), and sleep problems. The spiritual experience is creation at the divine level.

The Jade Gate chakra (also known as 8th chakra) is located on the back of the head at the occipital ridge—the pointy bone near the base of the skull. The color green transitions to black as you observe it. At the emotional/mental level, it is associated with perception of both physical reality and spiritual nature. These issues influence the central nervous system. The spiritual experience is perception at the divine level.

The Crown chakra (also known as Sahasrara chakra or 7th chakra) is located approximately four finger widths above the top of the head, and is represented by the color purple, and sometimes white. At the emotional/mental level, it is associated with spiritual evolution, and influences all other chakras. The spiritual experience is our own divinity.

We physically feel the energy, and our bodies and emotions (a result of physical hormones) are influenced when we meditate or receive energy work. Our human senses of feeling and mind make this physical and vital interpretation so obvious. We could be content with this explanation—energy flows through chakras. But let us look through the veil of this physical body and go deeper, to the level of consciousness.

Soul and Consciousness

The human experience of vital energy is real because we feel it. But it is also a tangible manifestation of the interaction of human and soul in the process of spiritual evolution.

I spoke before of universal life force energy—this chi (vital energy) is tangible consciousness. Consciousness is the state of being of paying attention, or being aware of one's self, while being aware that you are aware. Consciousness exists not only in the human/soul interaction—the simple mantra "Om" represents the entire universe, aware of itself. And we can describe a simple material object, such as a table, as consciousness with a memory, standing still.

From the soul's perception, the chakra is not an empty funnel or vortex made of energy, and the chakra system is not a hose through which energy flows. The chakra is a kind of membrane, like a speaker in a sound system, through which consciousness and states of being resonate. It is a sensory "organ" of the soul which extends into our human existence, observing the human experiences of happiness and suffering, and at the same time radiating the lessons of the soul back to the human. The resonance of each chakra vibrates at a frequency that corresponds to particular types of experiences.

The following diagrams reflect the resonance of consciousness through the chakra—the simultaneous transmission and reception between human and spirit.

Meditation which incorporates chakras encourages spiritual evolution because we are paying attention to both a particular human experience and the resulting lessons of the soul. This meditation is most powerful when we are in a state of self-compassion. Energy treatments affect us because the healer is in a state of compassion, and for some, a higher level of consciousness. This compassion and consciousness, along with attention placed at the chakras, influences the chakras. Compassion is where human and soul touch and influence each other—it is the true understanding which rises from experience (see the more detailed discussion about compassion in the section on R'shiNaya).

All of life is the result of, and is made of God, or Supreme Consciousness. Let us go even deeper, and higher, to the level of universal consciousness.

Divine and Universal Consciousness

You have now contemplated the chakra as a constantly turning subtle center of vital energy which draws universal life force energy into and through the body, affecting physical, emotional and mental health. You have gone deeper into the underlying truth that each chakra is a sensory organ of the soul, tasting the human experience and providing evolutionary lessons to the human. We began from a local human perspective, and then went deeper to the soul/human perspective, and this is still a local point of view. Now we go to the final origin of the chakra, the ultimate universal perception.

The turning or resonance of the chakra arises from the perfection and apparent dichotomy of being both human and divine at the same time. God is Oneness and Love, desiring to exist in a way to experience that Love. And so He generated an immeasurable force of denial which created separation (also known scientifically as the Big Bang). And thus He pushed Himself into individualized pockets of Himself. These individual pockets are the soul, each fully and completely God but each with its own unique perception that can now experience interaction and Love. And soul/God incarnates itself in physical form and lives the human experience.

God desires to be incarnate in the tangible world, and the soul yearns for Oneness once again. From the most subtle waves of energy to the highest level of the cosmos, there is love and denial. These forces of divine attraction and repulsion are consciousness turning on itself. This is the turning of the chakra.

Each chakra is a manifestation of universal consciousness, and although this consciousness may seem to exist locally in one area of one human body, there is the one chakra which exists everywhere. It is universal convection, the VishwaChakra ("*veesh*-wah *chah*-krah"). Allow yourself to sink into the experience of just one of your chakras, and you might feel yourself falling into the immensity of the universe.

Everything we perceive exists as a tool for our evolution. Thus the essence of this VishwaChakra can be felt and experienced in our physical bodies, energy, emotions and thought.

Contemplations on the VishwaChakra

As Above, So Below. The movement and expansion of supreme consciousness—from the highest level of the cosmos, to the chakra, to the smallest vibration of energy waves in an atom—is the same. It can be experienced in the Vishnu Shiva cycle as God's desire to incarnate, experience and evolve; in the first four Siddhis as the feeling underneath the cycles of life and nature; as the consciousness of natural forces holding the world together in Quantum Metaphysics; and in the many layers of the request for oneness and acceptance of experience in the Lord's Prayer.

The Vishnu Shiva Cycle

To contemplate the Vishnu Shiva Cycle is to experience the spiritual vortex of the chakras—the complementary divine forces that bring the perpetual motion, the "constantly turning". It represents God moving out of Oneness in the form of His creation, and the purification of that creation resulting in its movement back into God.

Begin your contemplation of the Vishnu Shiva cycle by reviewing the teaching below. Then do the first four steps discussed in the section on Meditation: in a calm and quiet environment, sit and breathe, paying attention only to your breath. Calm your mind, and pay attention inside yourself. Do your best to observe that you are aware of yourself. And now add the fifth step…softly contemplate the consciousness, and then let your thoughts fall away. Allow what might rise to rise.

VISH is the Divine intention to bring something from the Heavens (Heaven is everything and Oneness) into a transformation. The contrary force, SHIV, takes the transformation back to the Heavens. Maybe you have already noticed that "Shiv" is "Vish", just turned around. Vish is everything, going into transformation, while Shiv is the transformation that happens in everything.

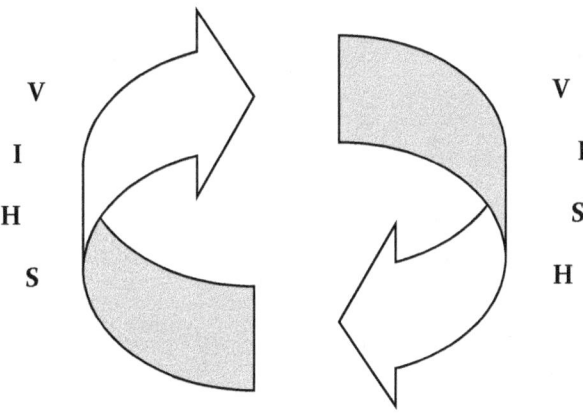

The letters "nu" express the consciousness of a densified experience, so Vishnu (what is Created by God, and what operates the Creation) is that universal thing that brings a tangible experience. The letter "a" represents the consciousness of the God presence, so Shiva (the interaction between Creator and Created) is the experience that transforms, that elevates and reveals the presence of God (see the section on The Ten Planes of Consciousness). The Vishnu is the universal experience, and the Shiva is the Love, constantly changing.

The Four Siddhis

The Siddhis are contemplative meditations on a single word which bring blissful states of being. The Sanskrit word "siddhi", meaning power or accomplishment, refers to supernatural powers that can be attained by the practice of yoga. The meaning of yoga here is the original one—a spiritual discipline that leads to a state of union with God. Krishna, an incarnation of Vishnu, taught the original yoga to Vivasvat as told in the Hindu holy book "The Bhagavad Gita". Eventually Patanjali compiled and perfected the teaching of the siddhis in the "The Yoga Sutras".

There are nine main siddhis known as the Continuous Path. Contemplation of the first four of these draws us softly into the experience of the VishwaChakra. Begin each of the siddhi meditations by breathing, paying attention inside, calming the mind, and observing that you are aware of yourself. Softly and slowly repeat the one-word mantra to yourself, eventually thinking it silently, while contemplating the consciousness described below. The italicized syllable in the mantras below indicates where to place the accent. After a few minutes, let go of the philosophical contemplation to remain in a state of awareness while you repeat the mantra. Come back to the mental contemplation only if your mind wanders, and then let go again.

Do this meditation for approximately 20 minutes per day, for a period of 33 days. You may skip a day here and there, but add this missed day at the end, so that you still do a total of 33 days. (Please consider and respect that we do not say the mantra aloud in any circumstance other than teaching or meditating—in conversation we might refer to the first siddhi, or the smallest siddhi.)

First Siddhi

The mantra is "anima", pronounced "*ah*-nee-mah". Anima means the smallest, most subtle, most refined, softest level of the universe, of energy. Take your time to visualize sinking into a single point smaller than an atom, the space between the atoms of your body. Contemplate what is the smallest in definition, density, frequency, and in scale—the absence of anything to compare it with. It is so small that nothing can cling to it, so it becomes free of everything. It is that very still universal substance that is everything and that is between everything, which is supreme consciousness. From here, all you can perceive is vibration, which is the sound of "Om". Here we become aware of the Creator.

Second Siddhi

The mantra is "mahima", pronounced "*mah*-hee-mah". It means all-pervading, immense, great consciousness. Expand into the universal substance which is composed of Love in five pure thoughts—the Five Elements, which together are the potential for all Creation (please see the section on The Five Elements of Creation). All vibrations and manifestations are experienced here at the level of galaxies and beyond. From here you perceive everything in the universe from the point of view of the universe.

This is the immensity of all of Creation—become aware of the flow of consciousness in a tiny flower, the same as an enormous star. With the first siddhi we come to a point of perception so small and subtle that immensity naturally reveals itself, and we fall into the consciousness of the second siddhi.

Third Siddhi

The mantra is "garima", pronounced "*gah*-ree-mah". It means the heaviest, densest, experience. It is a coming together, the compacting force of gravity, the combining of the potential for creation in the elements to become something tangible. It is the natural forces forming denseness and the natural world. The interaction of the Creator and the Created forms the mind, the heart, and the body. In the consciousness of the third siddhi we experience the densification of sublime love into tangible substance.

Fourth Siddhi

The mantra is "laghima", pronounced "*lah*-gee-mah". Laghima feels like the lightest experience, completely unaffected by natural laws such as gravity, or any outside influence. Everything is self-propelled from consciousness. Everything has its own free will—nothing is a force from somewhere else, and enslavement melts away. The movement of our hearts and awareness is not from natural forces pulling against our will, but from Love, because we want it. This movement is a flow without attachments—in this consciousness we are completely free.

With the first siddhi we exist in subtlety as universal substance, as everything, Oneness, with no definition or duality. From this smallest point of perception we fall into the immensity of the universe and experience the flow and interaction of the five elements of creation—second siddhi. With the third siddhi this potential densifies into incarnation and is moved by natural forces. And then it transforms and elevates, moving back into a state of freedom toward Oneness—fourth siddhi. This simultaneous experience perpetually turns on itself.

Quantum Metaphysics

Quantum metaphysics is the spiritual contemplation of existence, space, time, and free will as they relate to the scientific study of energy. This concept adds another dimension to the experience of the VishwaChakra, as it addresses the structure of atoms as consisting of energy, love and denial.

We have contemplated the movement of supreme consciousness at the highest level in the Vishnu Shiva Cycle, as the will of God to incarnate and evolve. We've contemplated this movement as the universal forces of nature in the first four siddhis. We've contemplated it as the individual chakra of the human body—the sensory "organ" of the soul which extends into our human existence, observing the human experiences of happiness and suffering, and at the same time radiating the lessons of the soul back to the human. And now we contemplate the smallest vibration of energy waves in an atom and the consciousness which holds the tangible world in balance.

To contemplate the Quantum Metaphysical perception of the VishwaChakra, review the teaching presented below. Breathe, pay attention inside, calm the mind, and observe that you are aware of yourself. Softly contemplate the consciousness, and then let your thoughts fall away. Allow wisdom to rise.

According to modern science, everything consists mostly of nothing. The atoms which make up everything can be measured as tiny bits of mass with huge distances of space between them. According to Newton's law of universal gravitation, every infinitely small bit of matter attracts every other bit of matter with a force that is directly proportional to the product of their masses and inversely proportional to the square of the distance between them—the part of this concept that we address here is that the greater the mass, the more forceful the attraction. So you could say that the earth attracts an apple a lot, and the "falling" apple attracts the earth, but not very much.

Everything is made in the image of God, is made *of* God. Love and denial move everything. At the atomic level, denial is a field. A point of balance exists where there is just as much denial around the atoms pushing them away from each other as there is love pulling the atoms together. Even within each atom, the protons and electrons stay the same distance from the neutron and from each other as they move with the pulling and pushing of love and denial. The electromagnetic force of love and denial pulls and pushes, keeping the entire Universe in balance.

But atoms are not solid. Quantum physics shows us that the particles of the atoms are not granular particles at all, but are waves of energy, which we know as consciousness. The neutron, which seems to be a tangible core of the atom, is actually consciousness, tightly wrapped on itself. The immense space between the atoms is consciousness, made of pure love. Our bodies are thus composed mostly of consciousness, in a state of Oneness—it is only these minute, few and far between atoms that hold the energy of separation and denial.

The Lord's Prayer

Jesus' disciples asked Him to teach them how to pray as He did, and He taught what we know as the Lord's Prayer or the Our Father. It is a prayer not only for the one who prays, but a prayer for all humanity as One. Rich wisdom resides in this lovely prayer at many levels.

The Lord's Prayer can be contemplated as a way to transcend in the universal chakra, the VishwaChakra. But each phrase also expresses an experience of the interaction of human and soul inherent in the individual chakras. This line by line interpretation observes the relationship of the prayer and the spiritual experience of the chakras—first with the universal chakra, then with the individual chakra.

Contemplate the Lord's Prayer one line at a time. Review the teaching presented below while focusing on the associated chakra inside you. Breathe, pay attention inside, calm the mind, and observe that you are aware of yourself. Softly pay attention to the consciousness, and then let your thoughts fall away.

Our Father who is in heaven

    Everyone and everything comes from the one Creator. He exists in heaven, which is the place where everything exists and transforms—from the subtle space between the atoms to the greatest immensity of the cosmos.

    The Void that is the total potential of the cosmos, from which everything emanates, is the experience of the Crown chakra.

Holy is Your name

    God cannot be named with a human word; in Hebrew, the word "name" is an archetype, or classical example of something that is not easy to understand. God is not definable, or specific to any religion or people. We each have our unique relationship with God. God's name is holy, radiating virtue. (See the section on Angeology for the teaching on virtue and vice.)

    An experience of the Third Eye chakra is everything you can conceive in your mind about God.

Your kingdom come, Your will be done on Earth as it is in Heaven

    You have moved and incarnated in our bodies, and have given us free will to experience love. Let us choose to be in service to Your will, and transform and move back to You in Oneness. *The VishwaChakra is most present in this phrase of the prayer.*

    The word "kingdom" is a symbol of the perception of reality, which is an experience of the Jade Gate chakra. "Your will" is the Word of God, His command, which emanates through the Throat chakra. "On Earth as it is in Heaven" flows from the Heart chakra, as the heart is where heaven and earth meet.

Give us this day our daily bread

Please provide what we need for nourishment and protection of our bodies and spirits (karmic experiences). We ask only for today, so that we may learn to live in Faith for our needs of tomorrow.

We receive nourishment in the Solar Plexus chakra.

Forgive us our sins as we forgive those who sin against us

Help us to accept that there is no offence, only experience which encourages evolution. And help us to forgive ourselves, in non-judgment of the illusion of our separation from God.

While we usually think of forgiveness as residing in the Throat chakra, this experience is about the responsibility of initiating forgiveness, which is the karma of the Sacral chakra.

And lead us not into temptation but deliver us from evil

Help us to recognize vice so that we may follow virtue. Help us find the faith, hope and strength to free ourselves from the suffering of expectations and attachments.

Temptation is the genetic reflex of desire which is an experience of the Sacral chakra. The Base chakra is the home of the base instincts of survival which push us to vice (evil). Both temptation and vice, although God-given gifts for survival, are causes of suffering.

For Yours is the reign, and the power and the glory for eternity

May we sacrifice our attachment to possessions (physical attachments of the reign), relationships (emotional attachments of power), and identity (mental attachments to glory) to You God, who exists without beginning and without end.

(There is no individual chakra association with this line.)

Amen—let it be, bring it here on earth.

Convection Mantra

This mantra expresses the experience of continual integration, and the resulting convection of purification and happiness. It has the feeling of the VishwaChakra, of what moves simultaneously at the level of our emotions and through the entire universe. The italicized syllable in the mantras below indicates where to place the accent.

Om hrim ram chakra prakshalana
Om hrim ram vishwa swaasthya swaha

Om	"ohm"	The universe observes itself
Hrim	"hreem"	Bija mantra of purification
Ram	"rahm"	Bija mantra of pleasure
Chakra	"*chah*-krah"	Constantly turning, convection
Prakshalana	"prahk-shah-*lah*-nah"	Purification
Vishwa	"*veesh*-wah"	Universal
Swaasthya	"*swahs*-tee-yuh"	Self-containment
Swaha	"*swah*-hah"	Surrender (of the human)

Take a few moments to breathe, place your attention inside yourself, and empty your mind. From this state of being, contemplate the VishwaChakra. Allow it to draw you in. Fall into it, and begin to chant the Convection mantra. You can softly contemplate the meaning of this mantra the way you did the siddhis, by repeating it softly and slowly. Or you can charge it by doing 9 malas a day for 12 days as explained in the section on Japa.

As thoughts and emotions rise, observe with compassion and integrate them. As they dissolve, observe with a great happy love for your ego which brings the opportunity to evolve. Feel the convection of emotion, purification and happiness, and the availability for the next purification. This convection exists both inside you and everywhere. Your integrations influence the entire universe because your soul exists everywhere.

Meditation on the VishwaChakra

This guided meditation takes your attention through each of the chakras, and then all at the same time, until finally you feel the one universal chakra (VishwaChakra) inside you and everywhere.

Breathe, relax, and clear your mind. As you breathe, feel the breath move through your nose, and notice the rise and fall of your abdomen. Place attention inside your body. If your mind is moving, pay attention to your breathing or chant the peace mantra "Om Shanti Shanti Shanti".

Pay attention to the sensation of vital energy in your entire body. You may feel a subtle vibration or warmth.

Pay attention to the Crown chakra... When you feel the vibration of the chi, stay there a while and experience it.
Now, move your attention to the 3rd Eye and spend some time...
Now, focus on the Jade Gate and sit there...
Now, become aware of the Throat ...
Now, the Heart...
Now, the Solar Plexus...
Now, the Dan-tian...
Now, the Sacral chakra...
Now, the Base chakra...
Return to the Heart chakra and place your attention there, and sink into it...

Keeping your attention in the Heart, also add your awareness to all the other chakras. It is an unfocused gaze, to feel all of them at once. Observe the Crown...add the Third Eye...and the Jade Gate...and the Throat...and the Solar Plexus...and the Dan-tian...and the Sacral...and the Base...The awareness of the vibration intensifies. Remember it is the dancing of ego and soul.

You are experiencing all the chakras at once, while living in the Heart. What seems to distinguish each of them begins to fade and dissolve. There is only one chakra in your body, and the Cosmos itself is consumed in this chakra. Release resistance and sink into the resonance of your energy. Allow yourself to fall into the immensity of the universe...the vibration of you is the vibration of the cosmos.

Spiritual Practice with Individual Chakras

Introduction

You explored the experience of the chakra from the more physical experience of the feel of energy, to the soul experience and even divine consciousness. And you contemplated the universal, all-pervading being-ness of the constant turning of the chakra.

Now we move to meditations which focus on what we perceive as distinct chakras. Every meditation will guide you into states of being of individual chakras. Each meditation might seem to be saying something different than another meditation about the consciousness of a particular chakra, but do your best to release your judgment—that natural mental response to compare and contrast the various wisdoms. Sink into each meditation, only contemplating that one practice, and let it touch you inside. The final section of this book will summarize the wisdom of these techniques for each chakra.

Hindu and Buddhist Meditation

Chakra Mandalas

Many Hindu and Buddhist traditions use lotus mandalas as visual tools for contemplation of the chakras as one of the practices of Tantra. The word "Tantra" comes from the root *tan* "to stretch or expand", and the suffix *tra* "instrument"—a tool for expanding. It has multiple definitions depending on which scripture one is studying—the two I prefer are a practice for obtaining spiritual enlightenment, and bearer of liberation.

Depending on the tradition, each mandala includes some or all of these representations: a significant number of lotus petals; a shape which corresponds with a physical element; a bija mantra; an animal guardian who carries the bija (known as the bija bearer); presiding deity; presiding goddess (the female energy of the deity); and a lingam (symbolizing divine male creative energy).

The number of lotus petals indicates the number of important nadis which emanate from the chakra. Each petal bears a letter from the Sanskrit alphabet—the entire Sanskrit alphabet (50 letters in all) is represented on the 50 petals of the first six major chakras. Like Hebrew, Sanskrit is known as a beautiful language of the soul because each letter has its own rich meaning. Each word has a dictionary meaning and also reveals a deep spiritual experience as we sink into the meaning of the letters. The individual letters resonate in consciousness, and in these mandalas, represent the subtle vibrations of each nadi. The entire world is reflected in the petals of the first six chakras, and the crown chakra of 1,000 petals represents all possible combinations of the 50 letters—the permutations of existence.

The Sanskrit character found in the center of the mandala transmits the bija mantra—when this syllable is spoken, whispered, or even thought, it vibrates in consciousness. The bija doesn't have a precise meaning, but brings an experience. The animal guardian carries the bija, and signifies that the chakra has the qualities of that particular animal.

To meditate on each mandala begin by breathing, paying attention inside, calming the mind, and observing that you are aware of yourself. Read the explanation of the mandala. Focus on the chakra inside you and gaze at the mandala. If you like, you may softly recite the bija mantra. Refer back to the explanation every now and then if you want to, and then go back to your chakra and mandala. Continue until you feel vibration in the chakra, an emotion or sensation in the body, or you find yourself coming back from transcendence.

Base Chakra
(Root or 1st Chakra)

- Sanskrit name: Muladhara chakra—it is the Root (mula) and Support (adhara)
- Petals and Sanskrit Letters: Four
- Shape: Square, the symbol of Earth
- Bija Mantra: Lam; the experience of incarnation
- Yoni: The inner triangle symbolizes the yoni (uterus) of Shakti (Divine Mother)

The Svayambhu lingam (divine phallus) resides inside the yoni and characterizes the male prime cause of the universe, which is Shiva. A snake wrapped 3 ½ times around the lingam symbolizes unmanifest Kundalini. When Kundalini sleeps, her mouth covers and blocks the opening to the Sushumna nadi. The elephant Airvata—king of elephants and vehicle of Indra (king of the gods, god of weather and war)—carries the bija. Here the elephant represents Ganesh, a deity who brings victory over obstacles and steadfastness in our physical and spiritual journeys. The presiding deity is Brahma, the Creator, and also Ganesh. The presiding female energy Dakini serves as the beholder and doorkeeper of the physical realm.

Human physical life begins through the tangible manifestation of divine incarnation in the Base chakra. God is present everywhere in the body, as is the potential for spiritual evolution. It is difficult to move our attention from the physical realm (the stable square) to the Self and then to remain there, but Ganesh makes it possible.

Sacral Chakra
(Hara, Navel, or 2nd Chakra)

- Sanskrit name: Svadhishthana chakra—the dwelling place of the Self
- Petals and Sanskrit Letters: Six
- Shape: Crescent moon, which influences the seas
- Bija Mantra: Vam, the experience of combination and unity

Makara, a crocodile-like sea monster, carries the bija. Makara symbolizes the waters, and is the vehicle of the god Varuna, lord of the sea. The presiding deity Vishnu preserves and operates Creation. The presiding female energy, Rakini, drinks ambrosia to exalt her mind.

We dwell in water, the womb of Divine Mother. Life and growth is supported in the Sacral chakra.

Solar Plexus Chakra
(3rd chakra)

- Sanskrit name: Manipura chakra—the Jewel City
- Petals and Sanskrit Letters: Ten
- Shape: Triangle, symbol of Fire
- Bija Mantra: Ram, the experience of definition

A ram carries the bija; this ram is the vehicle of Agni, the goddess of spiritual fire. The presiding deity Rudra, an ancient aspect of Shiva, represents transformation. Lakini, the presiding energy, is a compassionate form of Kali (Kali is also an aspect of Shiva—the experience of the destruction and transformation inherent in the cycle of time).

The precious fire of transformation burns in the Solar Plexus chakra. In a state of consciousness, our human self-definition begins to dissolve.

Heart Chakra
(4th chakra)

- Sanskrit name: Anahata chakra—Unstruck Sound
- Petals and Sanskrit Letters: Twelve
- Shape: Six-pointed star formed by two interlocking triangles, the symbol of Air and of the intersection of heaven and earth
- Bija Mantra: Yam, the experience of consciousness in the world

The antelope, vehicle of Vayu (god of wind), carries the bija; the antelope represents physical lightness. The Bana lingam contained in the Anahata chakra signifies consciousness and is the abode of Laxmi (Goddess of abundance). The presiding deity is Rudra or Shankara—both are references to the peaceful aspect of Shiva. The presiding female energy is Kakini, symbolizing balance between creation, preservation and destruction

Heaven and Earth meet in the heart, which is penetrated by the eternal all-pervading vibration of the sound of Om. There is a feeling of abundance, balance and harmony.

Throat Chakra
(5th chakra)

- Sanskrit name: Vishuddha chakra—Wheel of Purity
- Petals and Sanskrit Letters: Sixteen
- Shape: Sphere, symbolic of the clairvoyance of the moon; the element is ether, space or akasha; here earth, water, fire and air are refined to their purest essence and dissolve into akasha
- Bija Mantra: Ham, the experience of expression

The white elephant, vehicle of the god Indra or Akasha, god of the heavens, bears the Bija. The presiding deity, Maheshwara, signifies mastery over and union with the five elements. Shakini, the presiding female energy, bestows all higher knowledge and siddhis (powers).

Understanding of the unspoken word and the pure cosmic sound reside in the Throat chakra, and here Divine nature masters the physical world.

Third Eye Chakra
(6th chakra)

- Sanskrit name: Ajna chakra—Wheel of Self-Command
- Petals and Sanskrit Letters: Two
- Shape: Oval, or none; there is no element symbolism, as this chakra is beyond the elements
- Bija Mantra: Aum or Om, the experience of universal consciousness

The bija bearer is Nada, vehicle of the god of the mind—Manas. Nada represents the sound that fills the cosmos. The itara lingam resides in the Ajna chakra and holds the illusion of self and others (separation). The presiding deity is the half-male and half-female Shiva-Shakti, symbolizing that duality ceases to exist. The presiding female energy Hakini Shakti brings awareness of the unconditional truth of non-duality as she sits in perfect meditation.

Consciousness dissolves duality in the Third Eye chakra. However, we still experience this truth from a localized viewpoint.

Crown Chakra
(7th chakra)

- Sanskrit name: Sahasrara chakra—the Thousand-Spoked wheel; Wheel of Liberation. It's an inverted lotus facing into the body and Self, representing every level of consciousness as only one universal consciousness
- Petals and Sanskrit Letters: One thousand; the petals bear the total sound-potential represented by all the letters of the Sanskrit alphabet, fifty in each layer
- Shape: Formless, above the elements
- Bija Mantra: All possible bija mantras

Vindu, or void carries the bija. Vindu is also known as "bindu", the dot appearing above some Sanskrit letters. It is a supremely compacted and concentrated point of immense conscious power, the sum total of the potential of the universe. The presiding deity/female energy is ParaBrahman—undivided pure consciousness. Here all divisions between Shiva and Shakti are resolved.

The illusion of individual self is dissolved.

Divine incarnation creates human life and the potential for spiritual evolution in the Base chakra. Divine Mother in the form of water supports life and growth with the combining and dissolving movement of our karmic experiences in the Sacral chakra. Our human attachments are destroyed and we transform in the Solar Plexus chakra so that in the Heart chakra we exist simultaneously as human and soul. We find universal understanding in the Throat chakra, Oneness in the Third Eye chakra, and finally let go of any concept or perception of Self in the Crown chakra.

The Ten Planes of Consciousness

Meditating on the Ten Planes of Consciousness is a way of contemplating universal consciousness in ourselves. We exist in all ten planes at the same time, from the physical to the divine creator. But before we learn to pay attention inside, we are mostly only aware of the human planes because these are obvious to our senses. When we are in a very spiritual state such as deep meditation, our awareness shifts out of the human planes and into the soul planes—during this time we aren't conscious of our body. The purpose of this meditation is to stretch our awareness into human, soul and divine at the same time.

To meditate on each of the planes begin by breathing, paying attention inside, calming the mind, and observing that you are aware of yourself. Read the explanation of the plane and focus on the indicated chakra inside you. Continue until you feel vibration in the chakra, an emotion or sensation in the body, or you find yourself coming back from transcendence.

Divine	1. Creator
	2. Created
	3. Interaction
Soul	4. Consciousness
	5. Causality
	6. Wisdom
Human	7. Mental
	8. Emotional
	9. Vital
	10. Physical

The Divine Planes

The divine concepts of Creator/Created/Interaction are universal—every major religion and spiritual philosophy includes the essence of this concept. The Creator, Created and Interaction together make up the Godhead (or Holy Trinity), which expresses Itself through them. At these planes there is only Oneness. In the beginning, there was Void, and then it became conscious of Itself.

Creator

1st Plane—Crown Chakra. Everything comes from the first plane, the highest point in the universe. Catholics and Christians name the Creator God the Father; the Hindus call it Brahma; the Egyptians call it Osiris. Even the Buddhists have Amitabha Buddha—the infinite and conscious white light from which everything came. The Buddhists call His realm the Pure Land, the same thing that Christians call Heaven.

Created

2nd Plane—Jade Gate Chakra. The second plane is everything created, everything in the World. It is the tangible physical world as well as all potential for tangibility (see more about this in the section on the Five Elements of Creation). In this plane reside the most subtle vibration of energy and also the entire cosmos. No matter what one's spiritual philosophy, everyone acknowledges that there is something—Creation. And if "there is something", it has to come from somewhere—The Creator. Christians call the Creation the Christ, the Son of God the Father; Hindus call it Vishnu; Egyptians call it Horus.

Interaction

3rd Plane—3rd Eye Chakra. The Creator has a relationship with what He Created, and there is Interaction. There is movement and change, so there is transformation. Christians call this interaction between God the Father and Christ the Holy Ghost; Hindus name the interaction between Brahma and Vishnu as Shiva; Egyptians call the interaction between Osiris and Horus as Isis. This divine interaction brings transformation, collaboration, and evolution.

The Soul Planes

Whatever can be perceived about our self is not the soul, it is our human experience. The soul is not what is observed, it is the observer. No suffering exists at the level of soul, only experience. The soul exists in a state of pure, true self. The soul comes from divinity—it is permanent and indestructible. It exists forever and cannot be affected or altered by anything else but the Godhead—Creator, the Created and the Interaction.

Consciousness

4th Plane—Throat Chakra. Everything is consciousness, even the divine planes. At the fourth plane the consciousness of self as separate identity arises, the awareness of "that is what I am". Between the third and fourth planes consciousness pushed itself into individualized pockets of consciousness and soul was born out of Divine Mother. These individual pockets are the soul, each fully and completely God but each with its own unique perception.

Causality
5th Plane—Heart Chakra. In this fifth plane (also known as the Karmic plane) the soul makes available every experience. Experiences can flow from karma (the simple effect of a cause), or dharma, because the soul desires an experience. The movement seems to arise from an individual source, rather than the universal movement of the Third Plane.

Wisdom
6th Plane—Solar Plexus Chakra. This is the wisdom that the soul gains from the experiences generated in the Causality plane. It is not a mental understanding (it is beyond the intellect), but a feeling. It is gained through simple contemplation of what causes suffering and what causes happiness. The human desire to be right does not exist here, there is only observation. Wisdom comes from experience, rather than the transmission of knowledge.

The Human Planes

Our human experience is what we can perceive with our senses. We have thoughts, emotions, energy (life), and a physical body, all of which experience suffering. The human experience is impermanent and ceases to exist when the soul is no longer incarnate—when the physical body dies.

Mental
7th Plane—Dan-tian. Creativity flourishes in the Mental plane. Here our mind produces new thought about relationships inherent in the world and wants to express it. We see this in new scientific theory or in the arts of painting or music composition.

Emotional
8th Plane—Dan-tian. We feel emotion at the eighth plane. Intellectual learning also happens here as we ingest and memorize information.

Vital
9th Plane—Sacral Chakra. Our energy vibrates in the Vital plane (also known as the Etheric world) which is where we feel the chi. Chi exists everywhere, not just in our bodies. When the Vital plane—our level of life, energy and willpower—is hindered, we feel fatigued.

Physical

10th Plane—Base Chakra. The Physical plane is our experience of the five senses: sight, hearing, smell, taste, and touch.

At the 1st plane, there is only consciousness—it is not conscious of itself. In the 2nd plane consciousness manifests into something. In the 3rd plane, consciousness becomes aware of itself. Between the 3rd and 4th planes, consciousness pushes into individual pockets, so that in the 4th plane we are able to observe and pay attention from a localized point of view. In the fifth plane we gain awareness through experience, and in the 6th plane we know that we gained wisdom from the suffering in our experiences.

The soul brings the transforming effect of the 3rd plane of interaction to the 7th, 8th, 9th and 10th human planes to help us dissolve our attachments to possessions, relationships and identity (here it might be helpful to review "The Three Needs" and "The Three Attachments" found in the section on The 21 Masks of the Ego). Non-attachment is enjoying what we have, but being happy anyway if we don't have what we want—we can observe our emotions without drama. We become free to live our lives with the non-judgmental soul level perception of our experiences—and during the moments that we observe our experiences and emotions in this way, we exist in a state of enlightenment.

The Five Elements of Creation

God created the universe out of emptiness in the form of five elements—earth, water, fire, air and akasha (space or heaven). The Svetasvatara Upanishad, part of the sacred literature of Hinduism dating around 300 BCE, explains this perception of creation. This Upanishad also explains that meditation on the elements manifests their attributes in the body and brings healing powers.

God created the world in the form of Love, which can be perceived from five points of view—the five elements. Thus, the five elements of creation are not the physical elements we can see and touch; they are the spiritual potential for everything created, before manifestation in tangible form. The properties, personality, characteristics, and consciousness of the elements are something of what we experience in the physical elements, but not exactly. In the physical elements, we do experience their consciousness, but it is filtered through our human perceptions—we miss some things and add some things.

To feel the consciousness of God's creation, meditate on the five elements while chanting the elemental mantras. The italicized syllable in the mantras below indicates where the accent is placed. As always, begin by breathing, paying attention inside, calming the mind, and observing that you are aware of yourself. Read the explanation of the element and focus on the indicated chakra inside you. Then use the 9x12 formula explained in the section on Japa to charge the elements (bring their consciousness very strong inside you), which is 9 malas per day for 12 days in a row. It is important to charge them in the order in which they appear here as each is a foundation for the one following: earth, fire, heaven, water and then air. You can charge more than one at a time if you like, but keep the proper order. For example, if you want to charge Earth and Fire during the same 12 days, you would chant 9 malas of earth, then 9 malas of Fire each day.

All of the mantras include placing attention on Hindu deities; the Heaven, Water and Fire mantras also include Buddhist and Christian variations. While these mantras refer to Hindu or Buddhist deities, it is absolutely not required to be Hindu or Buddhist, or to feel you are praying to these deities while you chant them. Even when a mantra seems to be a prayer to a deity, we are simply invoking the state of being of that deity.

Earth

The Earth mantra is "Om Prithividhatu Bhumideviya" which loosely means, "Earthly nature of the Goddess Earth". Chanting this mantra invokes the concept of the divine nature of planet earth. The Earth element resonates in the Base and 3rd Eye chakras.

Om	"ohm"	Universal syllable
Prithivi	"*pri*-tee-vee"	Earth, the dirt
Dhatu	"dah-*too*"	Nature of; aspect
Bhumi	"*boo*-mee"	Earth, the planet
Deviya	"deh-*vee*-yuh"	Referring to a goddess (Devi)

The properties of generation (creation) and steadfastness prevail in earth element, along with protection and abundance. Earth allows the essence of things to coagulate; it establishes the building blocks of structure. Contemplating earth, we can feel movement that happens over thousands of years, like an incredibly slow-motion wave of water. There is steadfastness and peace in the movement. The steadfastness sustains intention, providing protection—we can say it protects us from magnetic fields, and from energy vampires. (Some people haven't learned to find radiance and self-love inside themselves—they are drawn to the radiance of others, and drain the energy they find there. This is an energy vampire.) So it allows progression without influence from the outside. The abundance comes from the continual regeneration. The feeling of Earth is clean and pure.

Fire

The Fire mantra is "Om Tejasdhatu Agnaya" which loosely means, "Powerful nature of Fire". This mantra invokes the concept of the divine nature of the Goddess Agni. The Fire element radiates in the Solar Plexus and 3rd Eye chakras.

Om	"ohm"	Universal syllable
Tejas	"*teh*-zhahs"	Energy or force of fire
Dhatu	"dah-*too*"	Nature of; aspect
Agnaya	"ahg-*nie*-yuh"	Referring to Goddess Agni

The consciousness of Fire is radiation, transformation and purification. Usually when we think of fire we think of destruction and suffering. But before there was matter or anything to burn, fire did not burn or destroy. The light of God or supreme consciousness infuses fire, and this radiance influences everything at every level. Every cell of a living thing, and every particle of matter, inherently yearns to elevate and be one again with God. Fire purifies, not by destroying something, but by elevating it to a higher nature. When a thing physically burns, it goes back to its most pure state. Nothing ever stays the same; change is the only absolute permanence. You can see this in the movement of the flame—it never stands completely still, and it is never in the same exact shape.

Heaven

The Heaven mantra is "Om Akashadhatu Shivaya", which loosely means, "Oh, heavenly nature of Lord Shiva". Shiva represents the concept of the interaction between God the Creator and Creation, similar to the Holy Ghost in the Christian tradition, and Avalokiteshwara in the Buddhist tradition. The Heaven element exists mainly in the Throat and Crown chakras.

Om	"ohm"	Universal syllable
Akasha	"ah-*kah*-shah"	Heaven, or spiritual realms
Dhatu	"dah-*too*"	Nature of; aspect
Shivaya	"shi-*vie*-yuh"	Referring to Lord Shiva

The Buddhist version of the mantra replaces the reference to Shiva with Avalokiteshwara: Om Akashadhatu Avalokiteshwaraya "ah-vah-loh-kee-teh-shwah-*rie*-yuh". The Christian version includes a reference to the most elevated Self, the Holy Ghost in BhagavAtmaya: Om Akashadhatu BhagavAtmaya "bah-gahf-aht-*mie*-yuh".

The heaven element is also called Spirit, Self, Void, or Non-mind. Heaven is the space in which the action of God—the process of elevating consciousness—is invoked in your life. Heaven is the pure true nature in all of existence. Heaven expresses itself in the unified quantum field of quantum physics, in the Pure Land of Buddhists and in the heavens of the Christians or any religion that includes the concept of heaven. It is that pure place where everything happens inside us.

Water

The Water mantra is "Om Apsadhatu Durgaya" and loosely means "Oh, watery nature of Divine Mother". This mantra invokes the concept of the divine nature of the Goddess Durga, of Tara, or of Mother Mary. The Water element flows in the Sacral and Jade Gate chakras.

Om	"ohm"	Universal syllable
Apsa	"*ahp*-sah"	Water
Dhatu	"dah-*too*"	Nature of; aspect
Durgaya	"duhr-*gie*-yuh"	Referring to Durga (Divine Mother)

The Buddhist version of the mantra replaces the reference to Durga with Tara: Om Apsadhatu Taraya "tah-*rie*-yuh". The Christian version includes a reference to Mother Mary: Om Apsadhatu Mariaya "mah-ree-*ie*-yuh".

Water expresses the feminine aspect of God, supporting life and allowing cohesion and dissolution. Water supports life, allowing everything to stay alive and to grow. All of existence is cared for and bathes in the womb of Divine Mother. The softness of water cools and soothes us. We think of water as flowing and moving things. Before substance exists, this fluidity comes from cohesion and dissolution. The consciousness of water allows substance to combine and separate according to every other force of nature. It's the glue and the solvent of the universe. This flexibility and adaption is the fluidity of everything flowing according to the will of God.

Air

The Air mantra is "Om Vayudhatu Hanumantaya", which loosely means, "Oh, airy nature of the son of Hanuman", and invokes the concept of pure mind. The meaning of mind here is both the mind and the heart—thoughts and emotions. The Air element moves through the Heart and Crown chakras.

Om	"ohm"	Universal syllable
Vayu	"*vie*-yoo"	Air or wind
Dhatu	"dah-*too*"	Nature of; aspect
Hanumantaya	"hah-noo-mahn-*tie*-yuh"	Referring to Hanuman

The Buddhist and Christian versions of the mantra replace the reference to Hanumanta with a reference to Perfected Mind: The Buddhist version is Om Vayudhatu Bodhicittaya: "boh-dee-chee-*tie*-yuh". The Christian version is Om Vayudhatu CittAmalaya "cheet-ah-mah-*lie*-yuh".

The consciousness of air expresses pure mind, communication, harmony and balance. When we think of air we naturally associate it with breathing. But before there was air to breathe, or beings to breathe, it is the concept of movement. Air is the element with the least tangibility or resistance, so substance moves through air. Information in the form of vibration flows or vibrates easily through air. Light waves and sound waves and odor move through air more rapidly and with less distortion than through water or earth. The air mantra opens the mind and other senses to a broader perception of the universe, freeing us from limitations. Air supports thought and communication of pure mind. This is why the Hindu mantra invokes Hanumanta, the son of the Monkey God, known for the swift, pure, clear mind—a mind that can focus rather than flying around everywhere. When the pure mind of air is in harmony, everything exists in a state of stability and balance.

God created the elements as the potential for all creation, at every level. All of the elements exist at the same time in everything, everywhere; they express different perceptions of the original creation—Love.

In earth we are aware of generation, steadfastness, protection and abundance; it is the building blocks of structure, thus where life and experience begin. In fire we feel the radiation, transformation and purification of what began in earth. With cohesion, dissolution, and soft caring, water supports life and transformation. The consciousness of pure mind, observing and understanding at every level, brings harmony and balance to existence and transformation. And this process of elevation of consciousness happens in Heaven.

R'shiNaya
The Hindu Holy Path

R'shiNaya (pronounced "rishee-*nie*-yuh") is a Hindu holy path. The Rishi is known as a see-er, a sage, or a saint. Three thousand years ago the Vedas (the oldest scriptures of Hinduism) were revealed to the Rishis while they existed in higher states of consciousness. Naya is conduct or behavior. R'shiNaya is the path to follow in order to become a saint, or see-er—one who has perfected his perception.

It is the exhaustive contemplation, a way of life, of five states of being—Peace, Forgiveness, Compassion, Gratitude and Mindfulness. The contemplation is a passive meditation: breathe, pay attention inside, calm the mind, and observe that you are aware of yourself. And then softly voice the one-word mantra while observing a chakra. The italicized syllable in the mantras below indicates where the accent is placed. The recitation begins audibly, but becomes slower and softer until the vibration of the mantra sinks silently inside. Contemplate the meaning given below and then quiet the mind's mental understanding, allowing revelation of consciousness.

It is a 10 day process. Meditate on each state of being for one day for 5 to 20 minutes, doing your best to have the feeling of existing everywhere (refer to the 2nd Siddhi). First day is Shanti, second day is Anuja, and so forth. This part will last five days. On days 6 through 10, meditate on each state of being as in the first five days, but instead of existing everywhere, place your attention on the chakras.

Shanti

The pronunciation of this mantra is "*shahn*-tee". For the visualization, breathe slowly and mindfully, imagining a soft blue light that extends from the 3rd Eye chakra to the Crown chakra. We call this "the breath of peace".

The Sanskrit dictionary definition of Shanti is Peace. The deeper meaning reflects the presence of the highest form of thought which transforms what is tangible in the world. Peace means much more than being calm in the midst of one of life's many storms. We experience the transformed perception that there is no war, there is no conflict—there is nothing to affect us.

Anuja

The pronunciation of the mantra is "ah-*noo*-jah". For the visualization, focus on the Throat chakra and see a blue light that extends from the Jade Gate to the top of the Heart chakra. The Throat chakra exists as both the separation between, and the understanding between, the divine and both the soul and the human. Residing here is acceptance that all is flowing. The Throat chakra is not a link, but an ever-open bridge and channel for streams of consciousness.

The dictionary definition of Anuja is forgiveness. The deeper meaning—true and higher understanding of a clear experience, is that an offense does not exist. We never did anything "wrong"; we never did anything "good"; we just did things. No one ever offended us; we only experience denial, ignorance and misunderstanding. We are the creators of drama, and we are the observers of drama. There is harmony between the part of us that experiences drama and the part of us that observes it. Anuja is an experience of universal forgiveness—we celebrate the perfection of God.

Karuna

The pronunciation of the mantra is "kah-*roo*-nah". For the visualization, observe divine white light in the Heart chakra. With each release of an attachment to our identity, the white light extends further outside of our body. The soul expands and becomes more powerful.

The dictionary definition of Karuna is compassion. Compassion does not mean pity or loving kindness. It is simply complete understanding of our own suffering and the suffering of others, (which may then lead to an act of kindness). The deeper meaning of Karuna is to let go and mourn our own identity and egocentric experience, our needs and desires, and our sense of self importance. Every part of our identity reinforces a fortress around our hearts, our hands and our sexual organs. The release of identity allows us to truly understand suffering and to contemplate that suffering is a dream based in attachments. We don't push away our identity, our loved ones, or our preferences; we simply mourn and stop holding onto them. We exert no energy to release anything.

As we let go of egocentrism, we can love simply for the sake of loving. The experience of enjoyment becomes more intense—food tastes better; relationships with loved ones fulfill us more, sex is better. When free from all the walls of our fortresses, Bliss comes and we are forever in a state of Oneness.

Krutajna

The pronunciation of the mantra is "ker-*tan*-yah". For the visualization, pay attention to an infinite blazing, golden, shining light flowing through the body from within the Solar Plexus chakra.

The dictionary definition of Krutajna is gratitude. Krutajna is not the gratitude we feel when we receive something we value—something material, emotional, or mental. This state of being of appreciation reveals that everything is wonderful and that we have everything we need, but the feeling is not fixed on anything. The deeper meaning of Krutajna provokes a change in our mental structure (from the flesh to the Divine part of us) toward gratitude for an experience. We feel a kind of non-dramatic amazement, being thankful for nothing in particular.

Manasvin

The pronunciation of this mantra is "mah-*nahs*-vin". For the visualization, focus on the abdomen, the Sacral and Base chakras. Be conscious of a presence sitting inside you. Consciously expand to everywhere, in everything around you.

The dictionary definition of Manasvin is mindfulness. The deeper meaning reflects intention invested in all things; the mind absorbed in every aspect of consciousness. We are aware of everything; we accept everything. There is no judgment or denial in our awareness.

Living as a Hindu saint is the diligent practice of perfect perception:

- finding no conflict in our lives brings peace
- releasing our belief in the existence of offence brings forgiveness
- complete understanding of our own suffering through the release of identity brings compassion
- living in a state of thankfulness for nothing in particular brings gratitude
- absorbing the mind in consciousness brings mindfulness

We practice these states of being during our experiences of ordinary daily life.

Kuji-In

Kuji-In ("koo-jee-*in*") means the nine hand seals, which refers to the mudras used during the practice. Kuji-in techniques were originally crafted by Indian spiritual masters of the lower castes as a method to expand consciousness—a purely spiritual practice. But with expanded consciousness, naturally follows the development of the mind, body and spirit, bringing supernatural abilities such as healing and influencing the weather. The wisdom was esoteric (selectively shared, or "secret"), so observers saw only the outwardly evident portions—the mudras and mantras, and were aware of the powers they gave rise to. Martial artists, sorcerers and healers took the evident, observable practice and made it their own, skillfully adapting it as a means of developing the particular powers they desired.

Kuji-in is most well-known now in the world of martial arts. Japanese warriors mimicked the sounds of the original mantra language of Sanskrit, creating their own mantras composed of Japanese syllables. These Japanese mantras carry (almost, but not quite) the power of the Sanskrit mantras because of the intent of the practitioner. (See the section on Mantras about the Sanskrit language.)

This teaching is of the transformational approach, the original spiritual wisdom. The short mantra presented is Japanese, and the long mantra is Sanskrit.

There are nine progressive sets of meditation, each of which requires the practice of five spiritual tools. Each set brings more refined levels of self-knowledge and revelation. The conscious concentration required to perform all five tools at once encourages rapid spiritual evolution—it is a path to enlightenment.

- Mudra—a hand position (finger binding, or finger weaving) that combines experiences
- Mantra—a sound, which can take the form of either a short word or a more complex prayer
- Focus point—where we place our attention (chakra)
- Mandala—an image that is visualized in order to engage the mind in active participation with a spiritual process (energy visualization)
- Dharma—the wisdom, the philosophical concept

As in the practice of the Five Elements, it is important to meditate on the sets in the order in which they are presented, as each is the foundation for the next. Breathe, pay attention inside, calm the mind, and observe that you are aware of yourself. Put your hands in the mudra. Place your attention on the chakra, and imagine and feel the energy visualization. Contemplate the philosophy, and then begin to recite the mantra at the speed of your choice, keeping in mind what it means. The italicized syllable in the mantras below indicates where the accent is placed. Continue all five aspects for about 30 minutes. Do the Rin process daily for about one week. Second week, do the Kyo process daily for about 30 minutes, beginning with one minute of Rin. Third week, do the Toh process daily for about 30 minutes, beginning with one minute each of Rin and Kyo. If it is too difficult to keep all five aspects going at once after you get started each day (this is normal when you are beginning to practice Kuji-in), you can let the philosophy and energy visualization fade to the background—they will still be there inside you. Keep the mudra, the focus on the chakra, and the recitation and meaning of the mantra.

Eventually, after enough practice, you need only say the short mantra in order to sink into the state of being of the set. This is why you might see someone practice Kuji-in by flowing their hands through the mudras and saying only the short mantra—"Rin Kyo Toh Sha Kai Jin Retsu Zai Zen". The detailed practice is essential to get yourself to that point.

Rin

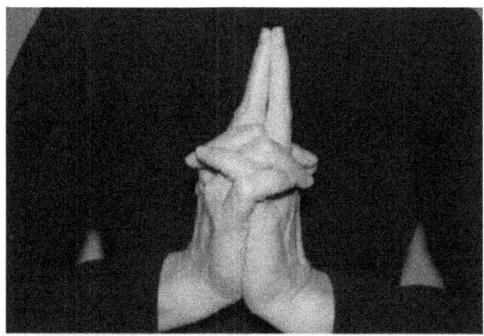

The meditations on the first of the Kuji-In sets, Rin ("rin"), focus on the Base chakra. Visualize a red shining light descending from Heaven, entering your Crown chakra and flowing down the Sushumna and touching your Base chakra where it lights a spiritual fire. This is divine incarnation, the powerful force of creation. As you breathe, each inhalation fans the flame and it expands, until eventually it fills your entire body. You access power and energy as you awaken your flame.

Contemplate that God always cares for you in every way, and that everything will always be fine. Let go of fear and worry, and be available to develop faith. This faith releases divine energy into the body and fuels all other spiritual activities. Rin means "to meet" with no reference to whom, thus we meet our Self. Here we sit in the Self, observing our self, being conscious. The Sanskrit mantra "Om vajra manataya swaha" means "I consciously exist as the Self".

The supernatural martial power of Rin is strength of mind and body, which flows naturally from faith and self-confidence.

Om	"ohm"	Universal syllable
Vajra	"*vahdg*-ruh"	Divine lightning; indestructible Self
Manataya	"mahn-uh-*tie*-yuh"	The result of being in the mindset
Swaha	"*swah*-hah"	Surrender (of the human)

Kyo

The meditations on Kyo ("kee-*yoh*") focus on the Sacral chakra. Visualize a white light simultaneously flowing in and out in every direction from the Sacral chakra. You circulate the energy in your body, allowing it to flow in and out.

Kyo is about responsibility, and means strategy or troops—we organize our actions to attain the desired result. We express this diligent behavior in actions, words, and thoughts—the highest expression is in the attitude of acceptance of our own mastery over our life. We cause every event and relationship in our life, what we perceive as good (happy) and what we perceive as bad (suffering). Let go of expectations that life will be easy and fun every moment, and be available to accept the will of God. The Sanskrit mantra "Om isha naya yantraya swaha" means "I use diligent behavior as a way of doing things".

The supernatural martial power of Kyo is direction of energy, which flows naturally from acceptance.

Om	"ohm"	Universal syllable
Isha	"*ee*-shuh"	Diligent
Naya	"*nie*-yuh"	Attitude, or behavior
Yantraya	"*yahn*-truh-yuh"	As a tool
Swaha	"*swah*-hah"	Surrender (of the human)

Toh

The meditations on the third of the Kuji-In sets, Toh ("toh"), focus on an energy area known as the dan-tian (the entire abdomen, or bowels). Visualize white energy entering the body at the dan-tian and filling the bowels with warm golden light—this technique gathers energy in your bowels.

Toh represents both "harmony" and "fighting"—when we stop fighting inside ourselves, we attain harmony with the universe. We accept life's events (Kyo), respond with forceless adaptation and remain at peace inside. However, we do take prudent action when necessary. The Sanskrit mantra "Om jita rashi yatra jiva ratna swaha" means "Defeat the zodiac, and reveal the treasure of life". The Zodiac is our personality, formed by astrology. It governs our human emotions and therefore our reactions to life's events. Let go of attachment to identity, and become available to inner harmony. As long as we have a human body, we will react—it is built into our cells. When you become aware of a reaction, look inside. Breathe, pay attention, feel the emotion without resisting, and then observe it; eventually it dissolves. (Refer to the section on Emotional Integration.)

The supernatural martial power of Toh is harmony with the universe, which flows naturally from inner harmony.

Om	"ohm"	Universal syllable
Jita	"*zhee*-tuh"	Defeat
Rashi	"rah-*shee*"	Zodiac
Yatra	"*yah*-truh"	Reveal, or bring forth
Jiva	"*zhee*-vuh"	Life
Ratna	"*raht*-n-uh"	Treasure
Swaha	"*swah*-hah"	Surrender (the human)

Sha

The meditations on the fourth of the Kuji-In sets, Sha ("shah"), focus on the Solar Plexus chakra. Place attention softly there, visualizing the area filling with a golden yellow light and pulsating with strength and peace. For healing, visualize this energy flowing from the Solar Plexus chakra to an unhealthy part of your body. See your cells as unhealthy, transforming quickly to healthy as you begin the chant the mantra.

Sha is about discovering the true power of the Self which we met in Rin. The power we thought we generated, and that we tried to control, is the power of God flowing through us. The control we imagined we had is only an illusion. We develop humility—not in the sense of feeling small and unworthy, but acknowledging that our power comes from God—and practice letting go of control. How could one harness the will of God? However, we have the right to influence God's power with our thoughts and free will. The Sanskrit mantra "Om haya vajra manataya swaha means "I ride on the mindset of the Self". Imagine joyfully riding a galloping horse—its power is not our power, yet we can guide it with the touch of a knee or the pull of the reins. Sha reveals stillness (absorption in Self) in the midst of movement (God flowing through us). Let go of human control and make yourself available to divine power. This power strengthens our ability to heal ourselves and others. It is limitless and omnipresent, dissolving our desire for competition.

The supernatural martial power of Sha is healing of self and others, which flows from Divine power.

Om	"ohm"	Universal syllable
Haya	"*high*-yuh"	Ride, or mount
Vajra	"*vahdg*-ruh"	Divine lightning; indestructible Self
Manataya	"mahn-uh-*tie*-yuh"	The result of being in the mindset
Swaha	"*swah*-hah"	Surrender (of the human)

Kai

The meditations on the fifth of the Kuji-In sets, Kai ("kie"), focus on the Heart chakra. Visualize the Heart chakra pulsating with the blue light of love—it perceives and emits everything in love, compassion and gratitude.

Kai is compassion, and allows us to feel everything. In Kai we contemplate that the soul is not localized in our own experience, but exists everywhere; we are everywhere; we feel everything. Become absorbed by the grandiose concept of absolutely everything. All we are is radiation and perception of love while in a state of gratitude. This awareness of Oneness develops compassion and unconditional love for our self and all things, manifested and unmanifested, accepting everything as it is without judgment. The Sanskrit mantra "Om namah samanta vajranam ham" means "I salute the all-pervading vajra" (what is indestructible and ungraspable). Let go of individuality and separation, become available to Oneness.

The supernatural martial power is premonition of danger, which flows naturally from Oneness.

Om	"ohm"	Universal syllable
Namah	"nuhm-*ah*"	Salutation
Samanta	"suh-*mahn*-tuh"	All-pervading
Vajranam	"*vahdg*-ruh-nahm"	The thing that is Vajra
Ham	"hahm"	Bija mantra of presence

Jin

The meditations on the sixth of the Kuji-In sets, Jin ("jin"), focus on the Throat chakra. Visualize being enormously tall, with a blue light emanating from the Throat chakra. "I have access to all the knowledge of the universe".

Jin is knowledge, and allows us to know everything. When we understand our self, we can understand everything. This self-knowledge is gained through inner observation and contemplation. The mind becomes still. It gazes on what we want to know, and we shed our human identity and preferences in order to listen to ourselves and others with an attitude of "I don't know". This perfect listening brings revelation, the conceptual thought of knowledge without words. Let go of opinions, and become available to perfect self-knowledge. The Sanskrit mantra "Om Agnaya yanmaya swaha" means "What Divine spiritual fire of creation is made of, everything is made of". When reciting the mantra, pay attention to the vibration of sound at the physical, vital, emotional, mental levels, and then beyond the human self.

The supernatural martial power of Jin is telepathy—knowing the thoughts of others—which flows naturally from perfect self-knowledge.

Om	"ohm"	Universal syllable
Agnaya	"ahg-*nie*-yuh"	What fire is made of (refers to Agni)
Yanmaya	"yahn-*my*-yuh"	Everything is made of
Swaha	"*swah*-hah"	Surrender (of the human)

Retsu

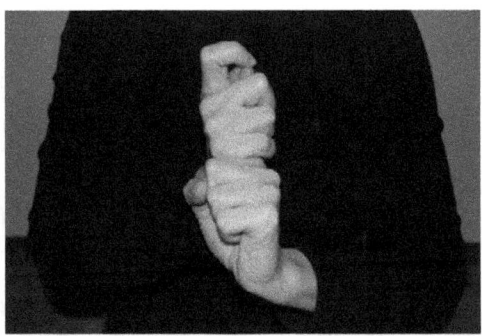

The meditations on the seventh of the Kuji-In sets, Retsu ("rets"—the "u" is dropped, almost inaudible), focus on the Jade Gate. Place the attention here, and contemplate that time and matter have no substance, all is energy, and EVERYTHING is timeless eternity. Allow your own visualization to appear.

Retsu represents perception. The light radiates through all dimensions and levels of experience from spirit to human. Practice at experiencing the tangible world as energy waves with a memory, standing still, rather than rigid solid matter. Contemplate that time and space are human structures—veils—that allow us to function in this world. When we let go of the control we exert on our perceptions, we can make ourselves available to be touched by the creation of God. The Sanskrit mantra "Om jyota-hi chandoga jiva tay swaha" means "Everything is a flowing stream of light, sound, and life". Let go of your beliefs of what Life is, and become available to new realities.

The supernatural martial power of Retsu is mastery of time and space, which flows naturally from clear perception.

Om	"ohm"	Universal syllable
Jyoti-hi	"*Yoh*-tee-hee"	Light
Chandoga	"*shahn*-doh-gah"	Chanting, or sound
Jiva	"*zhee*-vuh"	Life
Tay	"tie"	Flow, or stream
Swaha	"*swah*-hah"	Surrender (of the human)

Zai

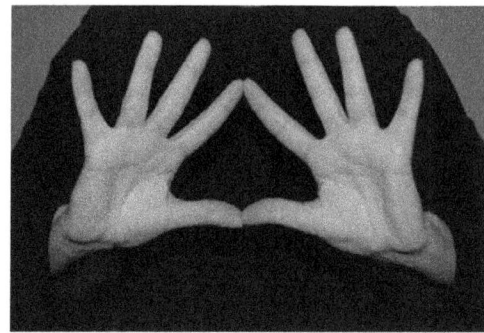

The meditations on the eighth of the Kuji-In sets, Zai ("zie"), focus on the Third Eye chakra. Pay attention there, and see yourself bathed in violet light. Begin by holding the mudra at the level of the Third Eye, and then slowly lower it to a comfortable position.

Zai is about creation and manifestation. We manifest powerfully at the level of soul, rather than ego. Let go of expectations, attachment and control. Sit in a state of gratitude and abundance, knowing that you influence the elements of creation (see the section on the Five Elements of Creation), which are the potential for all manifestation. The Sanskrit mantra "Om srija iva rutaya swaha" means I sacrifice my human self in order to create in the appropriate manner.

The supernatural martial power of Zai is control of the elements of nature, which flows naturally from the ability to manifest.

Om	"ohm"	Universal syllable
Srija	"*shree*-jah"	Create
Iva	"*ee*-vah"	Manner
Rutaya	"ruh-*tie*-yuh"	Appropriate
Swaha	"*swah*-hah"	Surrender (of the human)

Zen

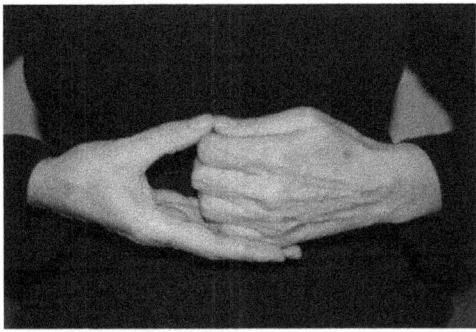

The meditations on the ninth of the Kuji-In sets, Zen ("zen"), focus on the Crown chakra. Place the attention here, visualize a calm white light everywhere, and then melt into it. Imagine emptiness. When reciting the mantra, pay attention to the physical body, then the vital body, then the emotional body, then the mental body. And finally, only to the consciousness inside you.

Zen is about "Absolute, or Perfection". The Self is unalterable; it cannot be affected. Pay attention to the Consciousness inside you, and melt into Supreme Consciousness. You are everything; you are everywhere; you are Void. Contemplate that your human, soul and divine states are all the same thing, just different frequencies of the same vibration. How could you be affected? Praise the Divine Spirit that you are. The Sanskrit mantra "Om arapacana dhi" means "To be anointed by the indestructible Self".

The supernatural martial power of Zen is suggestive invisibility, which flows naturally from the high vibration of Divine states of being (not obvious for the human to perceive).

Om	"ohm"	Universal syllable
Arapacana	"ah-rah-pah-*chah*-nah"	Cannot be affected, unalterable
Dhi	"dee"	Ointment

Summary

With Rin we pay attention and become aware of our soul, knowing everything will be fine. In Kyo we accept that we ourselves cause the outside events and relationships in our life in a state of being of responsibility. With Toh we look inside, bringing harmony to our emotional reactions. Sha brings the release of personal control as we feel the power of God flowing through us, healing us. With Kai we expand our soul perception from the local to the universal viewpoint, feeling everything in a state of love, compassion and gratitude. In Jin we develop perfect listening in order to understand everything in the universe. The divine level perception of Retsu allows us to see through the veils of time and space, experiencing everything as energy waves, now. With Zai we practice divine level manifestation by releasing attachments and expectations, and with our awareness of our influence over the Five Elements. In Zen we remember that the human, soul and divine aspects of ourselves are only one thing, and we melt into the universe.

The Cauldron Technique

The cauldron technique is used when we have a sexual desire that will not be fulfilled—either because the object of our desire is not available to us, or because we choose abstinence to further our spiritual evolution. The name comes from the visualization of boiling or burning the desire in a cauldron-shaped area of the body—an upside down triangle, or chalice, whose bottom point is at the Base chakra and whose wider top extends across the hips. Removal of desire is not the goal of the process, but it can be a side effect. The goal is to purify and elevate the desire, so that the energy invested in it will become available to universal consciousness.

Use your mind to provoke a desire to rise up in your body. Place the attention on the area around the Base and Sacral chakras, and chant "Om" loudly for several minutes. Extend each recitation as long as is comfortable before needing a breath, and feel each one resonating in the body. Be aware that this brings the divine into the body, allowing you to incarnate and be fully present.

Feel the fire energy in the Base chakra and water energy in the Sacral chakra, working together. Pay attention to the entire cauldron area, the chakras and the sexual organs. The loud chanting of "Om" causes fusion and boiling, amplifying desire. Breathe, inhabit, feel and observe (see the section on Emotional Integration). The sexual energy begins to transmute and elevate up the Sushumna.

Refer to the Kuji-In section here. In this practice, "Om" is integration. Chant "Om" at the Throat chakra (Jin) and the remnants of the desire continue to burn like fire. This fire moves and burns at the Jade Gate (Retsu); chant "Om" and perception transforms. It moves to the Third Eye chakra (Zai); chant "Om" to manifest the transmutation of the energy. It flows up to and out of the Crown chakra (Zen); chant "Om" and receive the higher wisdom which the mind cannot grasp.

The desire has become divine energy in the service of God.

I recommend a course on KamaChakra for those wanting to purify the suffering of sexual desire.

Kabbalistic Meditation

The Archangels

Introduction to the Tree of Life

The Kabbalistic system uses the Tree of Life as a mystical symbol to represent Creation and the workings of the Universe. This concept permeates every level of existence, from the universe, to the human being, to the atom and even smaller—"As above, so below". Through this study we seek to know ourselves and the Universe as an expression of God.

The Tree of Life tells the story of Creation. MahaVajra in his book, "The Seven Seals—A Practical Occult Experience", explains it this way: "The great light of creation came from the "Absolute light without end", and poured down like water to fill in ten spheres of existences, like jars. The waters of creation filled the first, then overflowed into the second, then overflowed into the third, down to the tenth jar/sphere. These jars/spheres are called "sephirot". The channels used by the flowing light of creation link the sephirot together and so permit the flow from one sphere to another. There are 22 of these channels, each represented by a letter of the Hebrew alphabet."

Each sephira is denser than the one before it. Five frequencies of existence dwell in each sephirah—the God form, the Soul, the regent/manager (or Archangels), the family of spiritual beings (or Cohorts), and the physical influence (after which the planets are named).

The Archangels

The Archangels express specific aspects of God. They are not individual angels, but the consciousness that we feel. We experience this consciousness not only in the general feeling of each Archangel, but also as virtues and vices. Virtues support the experience of Oneness, while vices support separation. Vices have been called sin, but to be vicious (to act with vice) is to act exactly as God created us to do in order to survive. For example, the greed referred to in the section on Gabriel (expending the least amount of energy possible to attain what we want) allowed ancient man to conserve his strength when food was not always available. In meditation, we associate the experience of each Archangel with a chakra.

To charge the Archangels, begin by breathing, paying attention inside, calming the mind, and observing that you are aware of yourself. Contemplate the lesson about the Archangel and the associated virtue and vice. Place your attention on the chakra, then charge the name by reciting 10 rosaries per day for 10 days while you continue to contemplate. This is different from the 9x12 formula we used with the mala. While 108 is a sacred number for Hindus and Buddhists, in Kabbalah the sacred number is 10. A rosary has 54 beads counting the spacer beads between the 5 groups of 10. So if you don't have a rosary, it is perfectly fine to use your mala—one mala equals 2 rosaries.

As in Sanskrit, Hebrew is known as a Language of the Soul because each individual letter has its own rich meaning and resonates in consciousness—this is the "deeper meaning" referred to in the following section.

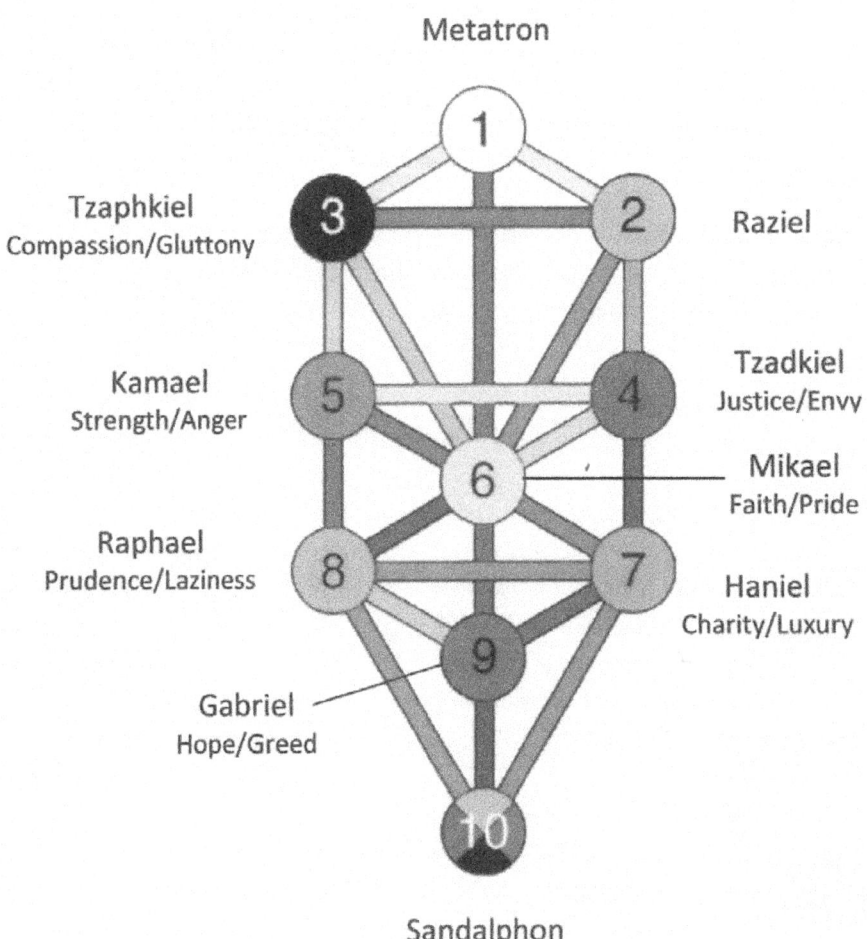

Chakras

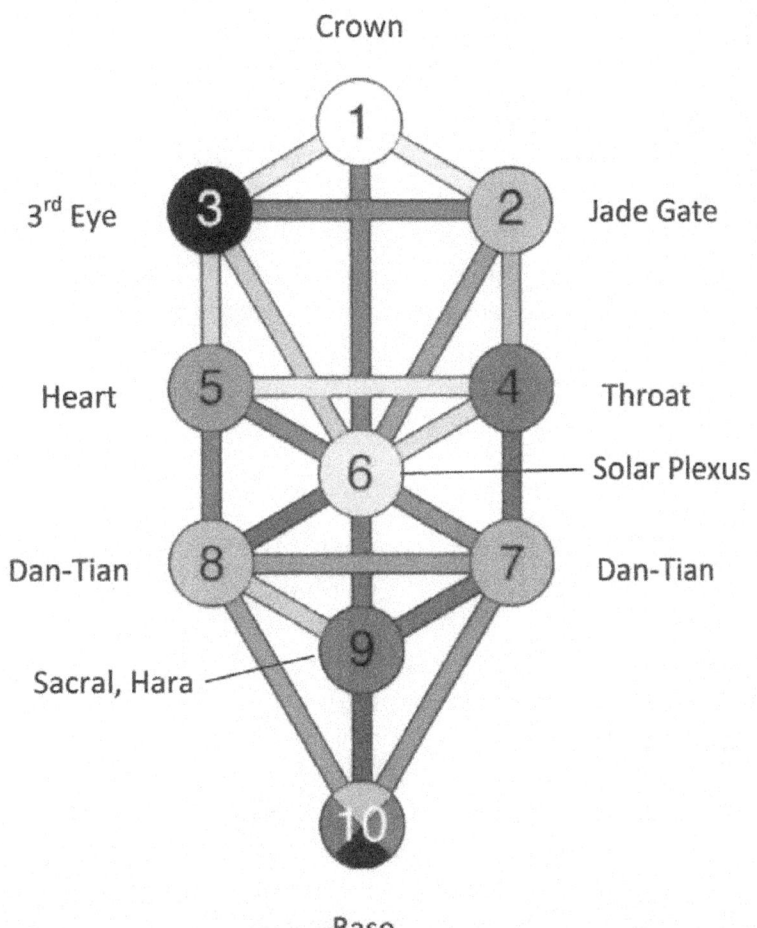

Metatron "Guarding the Law of the World"
Crown Chakra

The Creator aspect of the Holy Trinity is called Metatron ("*meh*-tah-trohn"). Metatron exists purely, fixed in unmanifested consciousness and stillness; with neither thought nor desire; in self-realization. Metatron defines the universe.

There is no virtue or vice association with Metatron.

Raziel "Mystery of God"
Jade Gate Chakra

Raziel ("*rah*-zee-el") is the Creation aspect of the Holy Trinity. It is what is manifested—Christ, Vishnu and Buddha. Raziel is how God operates the universe with highest intent, which is beyond human understanding.

There is no virtue or vice associated with Raziel.

Tzaphkiel "The Abdomen of God"
3rd Eye Chakra

Tzaphkiel ("*tzahf*-kee-el") is the Interaction aspect of the Holy Trinity, the intelligence of Yahweh, Shiva, and Avalokiteshwara. It manages communication, transmission, penetration and interaction. It inspires and enflames the virtues of other archangels. Tzaphkiel is to cause a divine experience of incarnation.

From the human point of view, Tzaphkiel is what causes us to want communion with God—to desire to be on a spiritual path, to desire virtue, to choose to be conscious. God begins to consider individualization in order to experience Love, and thus the interaction between Creator and Creation moves. Tzaphkiel is the Abdomen of God, the membrane around the digestive organs that holds everything while transformation happens. It is the mother's womb—Divine Mother, and VishwaShakti. Tzaphkiel cares for us and protects us at every level.

The virtue of Tzaphkiel is misericorde, or compassion. In Tzaphkiel we feel the pure and direct experience of Oneness that inspires compassion rather than denial. This elevates our point of view to take care of others. The corresponding vice is gluttony, which is overstimulation of the human animal at the emotional, mental or physical planes so we won't notice the suffering of our insecurity. This denial prevents our Soul from having a place to breathe.

Tzadkiel "Justice of God"
Throat Chakra

Tzadkiel ("*tzahd*-kee-el") is Divine Justice, meaning equity of rights. Tzadkiel provides for everyone to have an equal experience of the whole. In this state we experience both an absence of lack and an absence of abundance. Tzadkiel is what causes everything to be balanced and equal, to be set correctly.

The virtue is justice, the primordial feeling of the importance of what really matters. Everything that exists belongs to God, including our body and emotions, so may the will of God be done and not ours. We let go of yearning and accept equity. Our actions promote happiness rather than selfishness. We practice at releasing enslavement to identity.

Tzadkiel is also about rights and free will. From the divine point of view, everyone has the right to have what they want. This is not arrogance, but perfect freedom. We allow our self the freedom to do what we want without preventing others this freedom; the freedom of others takes precedence over our own.

In a state of separation, free will becomes self-importance, and then arrogance. Abuse of freedom is arrogance, which disregards the consequences of our actions. The associated vice is envy, which is yearning in an extreme state of self-importance. Competition pushes away the blessings of Tzadkiel.

Kamael "What is of God"
Heart Chakra

Tzaphkiel inspired Kamael ("*kah*-mah-el") with desire; this desire is what makes the choice. Kamael holds onto the focus; it is spiritual flame, and the steadfastness behind every spiritual empowerment. Kamael results from God wanting to incarnate; it is the desire to experience undefined love. Every human experience is caused by this desire.

The virtue of Kamael is strength to remain in a state of love. Kamael gives the strength to remain virtuous and holy and to cut attachments. It is to choose to disregard human preferences and pay attention to what the soul desires. The vice is anger—not being available to stay firm in love when things affect us, not remaining in a state of truth. It takes great courage to stay in virtue, rejecting materialism.

The mystery behind the strength of God is His love for individualized manifestations, knowing they are still not separate from the whole. And so we embrace our human existence, as God desires us to live.

Mikael "Who is God"
Solar Plexus Chakra

Tzaphkiel makes us desire to be on a spiritual path, and Mikael ("*mee*-kah-el") is *to be* on that spiritual path. In this state of being we are continually available to understand what is, or who is God. The entire universe feels it, this looking for divine essence. Mikael expresses the desire to discover divinity, something higher than ourselves in everything. Mikael is a universal questioning state, but there is no goal other than the question, "Who is God?"

The virtue of Mikael is faith, which comes when we are humble. It is not intellectual, but a feeling. We ask Mikael to guide us. If we think we find the answers to our questions about what is God, it can lead to certainty, and become the vice of pride. Pride is faith without God, in a localized state. Pride is our belief that we have the power to control our experiences.

We invoke Mikael in the six directions—above us, below us, to our left, to our right, in front of us and behind of us; and finally, inside us. This summons divine intervention, for when we produce the question inside, the entire universe answers.

Haniel "Grace of God"
Dan-tian

The consciousness of Haniel is enjoying God's creation. Haniel ("*hah*-nee-el") is the joy of being with God, and rejoicing in the simple things in life. Haniel is how God expresses himself through nature.

The virtue of Haniel is charity. We provide resources to others so they can enjoy that for which we experience gratitude—what we ourselves enjoy of God. When we feel grateful and act in charity, the universe bows at our feet and gives us what we really need. The vice is luxury. When we have more than we need, living luxuriously without sharing with others, we become enslaved to enjoyment.

A higher mystery of Haniel is forgiveness, which removes negativity. Forgiveness provides grace. We allow ourselves to accept the grace of God. We want to stop suffering; we want to rejoice. We make peace with our ego and enjoy ourselves as human beings. Forgiveness and sharing are the same experience to the Soul.

Raphael "God Heals"
Dan-tian

God brings a good way of feeling, and also protection. Raphael ("*rah*-fah-el") is defined contact with God. Raphael expresses appropriate communication, relationships, understanding and behavior that lead to a good way of feeling, without negativity. We find God in our lover and in the physical world.

Raphael's virtue is prudence, communicating and behaving in ways that ensure that everything is fine. We act with care and we pay attention—in a well-defined prudent manner. Prudence requires appropriate effort, but not perfection. Raphael is not about pressure or stress, it is the middle way. Have discernment about what needs to be done now, avoiding procrastination, and do it in a state of non-action (not being attached to the outcome) while enjoying life. To behave appropriately, or be prudent, is healthy. Emotional health delivers mental and physical health—we have the feeling that everything will be okay. Raphael's energy soothes and heals at every level, and naturally activates Kundalini. The vice is laziness, or inertia. Laziness provokes procrastination, and not having compassion for the result of not moving.

As we take care of ourselves and others, God takes care of us. We can feel God as a companion, thus Raphael is more intimate than Mikael.

Gabriel "Strength of God"
Sacral Chakra

The humility of Mikael densifies and becomes life, willpower and determination. Gabriel ("*gah*-bree-el") is like the camel, bringing the waters of consciousness into the desert of abandonment. Gabriel takes energy from the original source (God) and brings it to us. Gabriel is the feeling of divine power from God, incarnating in our bodies. We feel filled by the infinite resources of the Source. Everything we do, we do with God.

The virtue of Gabriel is hope, an all-pervading eternal optimism. We feel Hope about everything, not just about a specific circumstance. We feel the divine power. But when the ego feels the power, and says "I" am powerful, this is arrogance. The vice of Gabriel is greed, wanting and expecting everything to be given to us while we expend the least possible effort.

Gabriel is dense enough to be physically seen and felt. This is why Gabriel is sometimes called the "messenger of God".

Sandalphon "Residing in his Shoes/Feet"
Base Chakra

Sandalphon ("sahn-dahl-*fohn*") is the physical incarnation of divinity. Sandalphon is the final destination of God, where He wants to be in the physical realm, and why He created it. Every part of God wants to love every other part of God. God walks on earth-- Sandalphon is the power which holds form, and that permeates all of tangible nature. It is the laws of physics and chemistry, and it is consciousness—we can pray and it will answer.

There is no virtue or vice associated with Sandalphon. Everything above Sandalphon in the Tree of Life is meant only to accomplish that tangible, physical existence of God/Supreme Consciousness. When we live in the physical realm, we act with responsibility, prudence, charity, willpower, questioning, justice and righteousness; we do what is required to be compassionate. We act, speak and think in a virtuous manner, holding something so subtle as consciousness at the densest level.

The YEOUAN Technique

The YEOUAN technique is a Kabbalistic meditation on the states of being of the Hebrew vowels; this activates the chakras and incarnates soul and consciousness into the physical body. For most of us, in our normal non-meditative state only about 2% of the soul resides in our body. Up to about 10% of the soul resides in the bodies of the highest evolved beings.

The practice consists of toning each of the vowels as we contemplate a state of being and the chakra in which it resonates. To tone a vowel, sing it on one steady pitch for 20 minutes, loud enough to feel the vibration in the chakra. Continue each tone just until you begin to feel uncomfortable from lack of air, then take a normal breath and continue. Open yourself to experience and revelation.

- **I**, pronounced "ee". We focus on the area of the 3rd Eye chakra (the entire forehead) and contemplate the meaning of I—intention, the highest level of pure thought. Everything is born from intention. It is consciousness at the ultimate level, intention with neither expectation nor judgment. Pay attention to the 3rd Eye chakra, contemplate the meaning, and tone.

- **E**, pronounced as a long "a". We focus on the area of the Throat chakra, and contemplate the meaning of E—knowledge and wisdom. Every experience carries the wisdom that gave it birth. Every physical thing is wisdom, is the understanding of its self. Pay attention to the Throat chakra, contemplate the meaning, and tone.

- **O**, pronounced as a long "o". We focus on the area of the Heart chakra, and contemplate the meaning of O—everything, unified. Everything is an experience of everything, it is the whole of all things. We expand beyond the Universe. There is immensity; there is self-containment; and there is Oneness. Pay attention to the Heart chakra, contemplate the meaning, and tone.

- **U**, pronounced as a long "u". We focus on the area of the Solar Plexus chakra, and contemplate the meaning of U—experience (to feel, to exist, to live). Everything, physical objects and people, is an experience. Pay attention to the Solar Plexus chakra, contemplate the meaning, and tone.

- **A**, pronounced "ah". We focus on the area of the lower abdomen (the lower ribs to the sexual organs), including the dan-tian and Sacral chakras. We contemplate the meaning of A—presence, or being here, now. Everything, soul and consciousness is present inside you, resonating self-awareness. Pay attention to the lower abdomen, contemplate the meaning, and tone.

- **N,** focus on the Base chakra or the entire body. Contemplate a tangible, concrete presence made from the Universal substance. Sink into the body, and feel the density, the manifestation of the states of being. Pay attention to your tangible body and tone ("nnnnnnnn"). This consonant is not toned alone, but along with the vowels (see below).

Although the individual vowels seem to be different states of being, the entire Central channel from the 3rd Eye to the lower abdomen is one state of being. There is intention (i) of the wisdom (e) everywhere (o), which we begin to experience and feel (u), and everything becomes present (a). We embody this state of being with the consonant N, which brings manifestation of intention through presence.

The incarnation of the consciousness of the vowels is a 10-day process. On the first day follow the instructions given in "I". Repeat this process for each of the vowels, one day each for a total of five days. On the 6th through the 10th day, tone them one after another in one breath, adding an elongated "N" at the end, and focusing on the Base chakra or the entire body. "I-E-O-U-A-Nnnnnnnn". After you've charged this you can do it several times a day.

Summary by Chakra

Each of the spiritual practices reflects our experience of life as human, soul and divine. The chakra mandalas and Kuji-in contemplate that experience beginning with the physical Base chakra and following our evolution upward to the spiritual Crown chakra, while the Ten Planes of Consciousness and the Archangels begin with divinity at the Crown chakra and follow the process of incarnation downward to the Base chakra. The Siddhis, the Lord's Prayer, the Five Elements, R'shiNaya and the Hebrew vowels simply observe states of being.

And now we weave these treasures of wisdom together, observing and contemplating each individual chakra. Begin by breathing, paying attention inside, calming the mind, and observing that you are aware of yourself.

Base Chakra

Place your attention in the Base chakra and contemplate.

- The Lord's Prayer requests our Father to "Deliver us from evil". This evil is vice—the way we behave as a result of the God-given gift of survival instincts—which is a cause of suffering.
- The mandala of Earth reveals divine incarnation creating human life in the form of divine phallus and uterus. The sleeping Kundalini shows the potential for our spiritual evolution, which Ganesh makes possible by dissolving inertia.
- Our human tangible experience of the five senses—touch, sight, smell, hearing, and taste—sits in the Physical plane of consciousness.
- The Earth element allows the coagulation of essences for generation. It moves with steadfastness; it protects; and it feels of abundance and peace.
- The holy state of being of Manasvin is mindfulness. Absorbed in consciousness, the non-judgmental mind invests intention in all things with awareness and acceptance.
- The Rin kuji shows divine incarnation through a red shining light descending from Heaven to light a spiritual fire in the Base chakra. This precious gift of consciousness brings awareness of Self and God's constant caring for us. Let go of fear, and allow faith.
- Divinity incarnates in Archangel Sandalphon, the power holding form that permeates all of tangible nature. Sandalphon is consciousness at the densest level, allowing divinity to walk on earth.
- Toning the "nnnnn" along with the Hebrew vowels densifies and brings states of being into the body: pure thought absent of judgment, the understanding that everything is wisdom, Oneness, the experience of feeling and living, and the presence of here and now.

Life and the potential for our own Self-aware spiritual evolution begin. God both expresses Himself and observes that expression in the physical body.

Sacral Chakra

Place your attention in the Sacral chakra and contemplate.

- "Forgive us our sins as we forgive those who sin against us" from the Lord's Prayer expresses the karmic responsibility for initiating forgiveness. And from the phrase "Lead us not into temptation", temptation refers to the genetic reflex of desire which is a cause of suffering.
- The mandala of Water expresses the Self dwelling in the womb of Divine Mother. Vishnu operates Creation, and Divine Mother cares for it.
- We feel chi in the Vital plane of consciousness. Energy, life and willpower exist here.
- The feminine aspect of God flows in the Water element, which pervades the entire universe. The womb of Divine Mother cares for us and supports life with the aspects of cohesion and dissolution.
- As in the Base chakra, the holy state of being of Manasvin is mindfulness. Absorbed in consciousness, the non-judgmental mind invests intention in all things with awareness and acceptance.
- The Kyo visualization of energy simultaneously flowing in and out of the Sacral chakra represents our responsibility for creating our life experiences. Contemplate karma, dissolve resistance, and learn from each experience. Let go of expectations, allowing acceptance and appreciation.
- Archangel Gabriel, the Strength of God, is the consciousness of the virtue of Hope—an eternal optimism—as well as life, willpower and determination. Gabriel brings into us the energy of God and the waters of consciousness.
- The Hebrew vowel "a" is the awareness of the presence of consciousness inside you.

We consciously exist in the womb of the cosmos where all-pervading Divine Mother cares for us. We accept responsibility for our life experience with Hope. Life energy, willpower, and sexual desire reside here.

The Dan-tian

Place your attention in the dan-tian and contemplate.

- We feel emotion and perform intellectual learning (memorization) in the Emotional plane of consciousness; the creative mind flourishes in the Mental plane of consciousness.
- The Toh kuji of Harmony leads us to loosen the hold of attachment to our identity and preferences, and thus master our reactions to life so that we are at peace inside. Inner harmony becomes outer harmony.
- Archangel Haniel, the "Grace of God", expresses the complete and free joy of God's gifts of His expression in nature. The virtue of Haniel is Charity, sharing with others what we ourselves enjoy. Archangel Raphael, "God Heals", is defined contact with God and fosters the kind of communication and relationships in which we find God. The virtue of Raphael is Prudence, doing what is required so that everything will be fine, but without undue stress. We feel God as a companion in everything.
- The Hebrew vowel "a" is the consciousness of presence, the self-awareness of consciousness inside us.

We emotionally and mentally experience God's expression in the world, and joyfully share God's bounty. In a state of inner harmony we let go of our attachment to human identity and preference. We do everything with God; we act with prudence.

Solar Plexus Chakra

Place your attention in the Solar Plexus chakra and contemplate.

- "Give us this day our daily bread" from the Lord's Prayer reminds us to live in a state of Faith, acknowledging that all physical and spiritual nourishment comes from God, and always will.
- The mandala of the Jewel City reflects the precious, radiant nature of Fire—the transformation that is our spiritual evolution.
- Truth resides in the Wisdom plane of consciousness. Wisdom comes from the contemplation of what causes suffering and what causes happiness in each experience.
- The consciousness of the Fire element is radiance, transformation, purification and elevation.
- The holy state of being of Krutajna is an all-pervading gratitude, not fixed on anything. In abundance, we have everything we need.
- The Sha kuji brings great power and healing abilities. We let go of the illusion of human control we have in our lives and make ourselves available to divine power. There is no need for competition. Feel the movement in non-movement.
- Archangel Mikael, ever-questioning "Who is God?" is the presence of Faith. Mikael is to humbly be on a spiritual path, looking to discover God but with no goal other than the question.
- Tone the Hebrew vowel "u", experiencing living, feeling and existing. Contemplate that everything is experience.

The radiance of God brings spiritual transformation—the wisdom which rises out of suffering. The perception of human identity transforms into Faith, acknowledging that all power and experience is of God. We search for all expressions of God in a state of Faith and Gratitude.

Heart Chakra

Place your attention in the Heart chakra and contemplate.

- "On Earth as it is in Heaven" from the Lord's Prayer observes the heart as the meeting of heaven and earth.
- We feel the eternal all-pervading vibration of the sound of Om in the Unstruck Sound mandala. Here everything flows through air in a state of consciousness and harmony.
- The Soul manifests every life experience in the Causality, or Karmic, plane of consciousness.
- Air, the least tangible of the elements, supports unhindered movement, communication and understanding. The perfected pure mind brings harmony, stability and balance.
- The Holy state of being of Karuna, or Compassion, brings complete understanding of suffering and the resulting non-attachment. Cutting the attachments we have to our own identity allows this experience.
- The Sha kuji guides us, in a state of compassion and gratitude, to perceive everything as Love, and that our only opinion of each experience is to be in a state of Love. We see that the distinction between ourselves and others is illusion, allowing Oneness.
- Archangel Kamael, "What is of God", is God's desire to experience undefined love. Here stands the virtue of Strength to remain in a state of Love and to cut attachments.
- Tone the Hebrew vowel "o", contemplating the whole of all things. Everything is an experience of everything in Oneness.

Heaven and earth meet in the Heart chakra. Here we experience everything in a state of undefined love, compassion and harmony, allowing the consciousness of Oneness.

Throat Chakra

Place your attention in the Throat chakra and contemplate.

- "Your will be done" from the Lord's Prayer reflects the emanation of the Word of God, of His command.
- The mandala of the Wheel of Purity represents Heaven and the expression of divine nature mastering physical nature. Understanding of pure cosmic sound and the unspoken word comes.
- The self-aware Soul begins its existence as individualized God consciousness in the plane of Consciousness.
- The Heaven element provokes the action of God in our lives and is the place where transformation happens. It is the pure true nature in all existence.
- The Holy state of Anuja, or Forgiveness, bridges understanding between the divine and both the soul and human; streams of consciousness flow here. Harmony between the part of us that experiences drama and the part that observes it leads to the understanding that an offense does not exist.
- With the Jin kuji we have access to all the knowledge of the universe through perfect self-knowledge, even knowing the thoughts of others. Letting go of opinions in the vulnerable state of "I don't know" brings revelation.
- Archangel Tzadkiel, "Justice of God", causes everything to be balanced and equal. The virtue of Divine Justice comes from everything belonging to God. Contemplate releasing identity to feel the global perspective of Justice.
- Tone the Hebrew vowel "e", contemplating the knowledge and wisdom that birthed everything.

God individualizes and is aware of Himself as Soul. The pure thought of divine intention communicates with the soul and human, bringing revelation to the vulnerable mind and transformation of perception—the understanding that offense does not exist, and that God's creation is perfectly equitable and balanced. Forgiveness transforms everything.

Third Eye Chakra

Place your attention in the Third Eye chakra and contemplate.

- In the Lord's Prayer "Holy is Your Name" expresses everything you can conceive in your mind about God.
- The mandala of Self Command reflects absorption in Self, the perfect meditation in which consciousness dissolves the perception of duality.
- In the Interaction plane of consciousness the Creator has a relationship with what He created, bringing transformation, collaboration, and evolution. God begins to consider individualization in order to experience Love, and thus the interaction between Creator and Created moves.
- The Earth element allows the coagulation of essences for generation. It moves with steadfastness; it protects; and it feels of abundance and peace. The consciousness of Fire is radiance, transformation and purification. The collaboration of these elements brings manifestation.
- The Holy state of being of Shanti, or Peace, is the presence of the highest form of thought which transforms perception. Conflict does not exist, nothing can affect me.
- With the Zai kuji we manifest at the level of Soul by influencing the elements. Let go of expectations, attachments, and control while gazing on what you want.
- Archangel Tzaphkiel, the "Abdomen of God" is the inspiration and desire to be on a spiritual path, to choose to be virtuous, conscious, and compassionate.
- Contemplate divine intention—the highest level of pure thought, intention without judgment—while toning the Hebrew vowel "i".

Contemplate how God moves and interacts with what He created; the pure thought of God—thought without attachment or judgment—initiates the movement. Here the soul and divine manifest with generation and transformation, influencing the potential for everything. Transformed perception finds no conflict, and there is peace. Feel the desire to move on the spiritual path.

Jade Gate Chakra

Place your attention in the Jade Gate and contemplate.

- The word "kingdom" from the phrase "Your kingdom come" in the Lord's Prayer symbolizes the perception of reality.
- The Created plane of consciousness is everything created, from the most subtle vibration of energy to the immensity of the cosmos; both tangibility and the potential for tangibility.
- The feminine aspect of God flows in the water element, which pervades the entire universe. The womb of Divine Mother cares for us and supports life with the aspects of cohesion and dissolution—in non-attachment, everything flows with the will of God.
- With the Retsu kuji we practice at perceiving all information with non-distinction—waves of energy without the parameters of time and space. When we pay attention, apparent solidity, colors, smells, and music all become the joyful miracle of God's creation. Let go of beliefs in what the world is, and become available to new realities.
- Archangel Raziel, the "Mystery of God", is beyond human understanding. It is what God created and how he operates it.

All of Creation, from the most subtle to the most immense, from the intangible to the tangible, is supported in the womb of Divine Mother. Comprehend the mystery of God by releasing attachment to human perception; be available to observe life experiences while gazing in a state non-distinction.

Crown Chakra

Place your attention in the Crown chakra and contemplate.

- "Our Father who is in Heaven" of the Lord's Prayer refers to the Void that is the total potential of the cosmos, from which everything emanates.
- The inverted lotus mandala is the Thousand-Spoked wheel, the Wheel of Liberation. The immense conscious power that is the sum total of the potential of the universe dissolves the illusion of the individual Self.
- The highest point of consciousness from which everything comes exists in the Creator plane.
- Air, the least tangible of the elements, supports unhindered movement, communication and understanding. The perfected pure mind brings harmony, stability and balance.
- The Holy state of being of Shanti, or Peace, expresses the presence of the highest form of thought which transforms perception. There is no conflict.
- The practice of the Zen kuji of Perfection melts us into the universe. We embody the human, soul and divine natures, becoming aware that all is consciousness; each is simply a different frequency of the universal vibration. Nothing affects us.
- Archangel Metatron, "Guarding the Law of the World", is unmanifested consciousness which defines the universe. Be fixed in stillness with no thought or desire.

Everything emanates from the Void that is the total potential of the cosmos. Fixed in stillness, we find no difference between divine, soul, and human. With a perfected mind, even the perception of individual point of view fades away and we melt into the universe.

Conclusion

Through this esoteric spiritual experience of chakras, you have tools with which to contemplate our simultaneous existence as human, soul and divine; to feel the essence of each individual chakra even as they blend together imperceptibly like the colors of the rainbow; and to expand your perception to encompass the one local and universal perspective, which is God at every level.

At the human level we experience the chakra as a whirling subtle center of vital energy which draws universal life force energy into and through the body, affecting physical, emotional and mental health. At a deeper level, the chakra is a sensory organ of the soul, tasting the human experience and providing evolutionary lessons. Even deeper, divine incarnation and the yearning of everything in the cosmos for a return to Oneness drive the perpetual movement of the universe.

By allowing the consciousness of these teachings to affect you, wisdom transforms your perception and you experience the awakening of your chakras.

"The Soul wants to be in love with God…If you never address yourself to something beyond your human, you will stay just a human." ~MahaVajra~

References

The Teachings of MahaVajra (www.mahavajra.com)

Books:
- Conquering Drama
- Develop ESP and Supernatural Abilities
- Kuji-In 2, Advanced Kuji-In
- Kuji-In 3, Kuji-In Mastery
- Quantum Buddhism
- The Seven Seals—A Practical Occult Experience

Videos:
- Angeology, Invoking the Archangels
- Atma Yoga, Divine Incarnation of the Soul
- Creative Forces Seminar, The Language of the Soul
- Emotional Blocks and Chains, Freedom through Emotional Integration
- Kuji-In Video Training Kit
- Quantum Metaphysics
- Secrets of the Ego
- Seeing Through the Veil
- Siddhi Meditation

www.ingramcontent.com/pod-product-compliance
Lightning Source LLC
Chambersburg PA
CBHW081841170426
43199CB00017B/2806